I love you New Zealand

101 MUST-DO'S FOR KIWIS

Editor: John McCrystal

RANDOM HOUSE
NEW ZEALAND

National Library of New Zealand Cataloguing-in-Publication Data
McCrystal, John.
I love you New Zealand : 101 must do's for Kiwis / AA ; John
McCrystal.
Includes index.
ISBN 978-1-86941-899-1
1. New Zealand— Description and travel. I. Automobile
Association (N.Z.) II. Title.
919.3—dc 22

A RANDOM HOUSE BOOK
published by
Random House New Zealand
18 Poland Road, Glenfield, Auckland, New Zealand
www.randomhouse.co.nz

Random House International
Random House
20 Vauxhall Bridge Road
London, SW1V 2SA
United Kingdom

Random House Australia (Pty) Ltd
20 Alfred Street, Milsons Point, Sydney,
New South Wales 2061, Australia

Random House South Africa Pty Ltd
Isle of Houghton
Corner Boundary Road and Carse O'Gowrie
Houghton 2198, South Africa

Random House Publishers India Private Ltd
301 World Trade Tower, Hotel Intercontinental Grand Complex,
Barakhamba Lane, New Delhi 110 001, India

First published 2007. Reprinted 2007 (twice), 2008 (twice)

© 2007 New Zealand Automobile Association

ISBN 978 1 86941 899 1

Cover and text design: Nick Turzynski, redinc

Front cover illustrations
Right from top: Roberton Island/Destination Northland; Coronet Peak/Miles Holden; Mitre Peak/Destination Fiordland; Mount Maunganui/Bay of Plenty Tourism; Mount Maunganui/Bay of Plenty Tourism.
Back cover illustrations
From top: Cape Reinga/Janet Lewis; Hundertwasser Toilets/Destination Northland; Queenstown/A. J. Hackett; Fox Glacier/ Fox Glacier Guiding.

Printed in China by Everbest

Contents

Top 20 Must-do's

Over 195,500 people voted for their favourite must-do experience resulting in the following top 20 must-do's for Kiwis.

1. Mitre Peak & Milford Sound
2. Doubtful Sound
3. Bay of Islands
4. Fiordland National Park
5. Abel Tasman National Park
6. Aoraki/Mount Cook
7. Coastal Kaikoura
8. Hanmer Springs
9. Camping Country
10. Tutukaka/The Poor Knights
11. Marlborough Sounds
12. Fox and Franz Josef Glaciers
13. Ruapehu, Ngauruhoe & Tongariro
14. Waitomo Caves
15. Southern Scenic Route
16. Otago Rail Experience
17. White Island
18. Stewart Island
19. Arthur's Pass National Park
20. Tongariro Crossing

Introduction

New Zealanders are proud of their country. In fact, parochialism is a Kiwi staple and our level of insecurity with regard to international visitors' opinions of New Zealand can be almost embarrassing. ('What do you think of New Zealand? Oh, you haven't even left the airport yet. Well, what do you think of it anyway?') Yes, it is true: 'We love you New Zealand!'

Such is our fervour that one could ask why Kiwis are so prone to departing on overseas holidays and why many New Zealanders have not explored our spectacular nation at all.

Recognising that it was time to remind ourselves of the great experiences our country has to offer, the Automobile Association decided to highlight some of the sensational destinations and activities to be found in New Zealand. Similarly, we wanted to encourage tourists from overseas to visit some of the less well-known places loved by Kiwis. We didn't realise the fun we would have in drawing up a list of 101 must-do's for Kiwis or, for that matter, the debate we would start and the controversy we would cause.

Who better than the locals to recommend their favourite places and experiences in New Zealand? The Regional Tourism Organisations put forward their nominations from their own areas and from these the list of 101 must-do's was drawn up. Kiwis from around the country were then invited to vote for their favourite must-do's and also to suggest other places or experiences they thought deserved to be on the list — the 102s. And vote they did. The response was amazing. We received more than six million hits on the AA website in the five months of voting. We have included in this book some of the enthusiastic comments about the 101 must-do's and some of the wonderful suggestions that were made for 102s.

I hope that you enjoy your journey through New Zealand and that this book reinvigorates your desire to explore.

A great New Zealand experience may be just around the corner . . .

Peter Blackwell
Automobile Association

101 MUST-DO'S FOR KIWIS

Northland

It's the winterless north of the country, with some of the best beaches in the world strung along its east coast, and surfing, diving, fishing and boating opportunities galore. Northland is home to mystical Cape Reinga, the mighty kauri of Waipoua, the birthplace of the nation at Waitangi and New Zealand's most interesting public toilet.

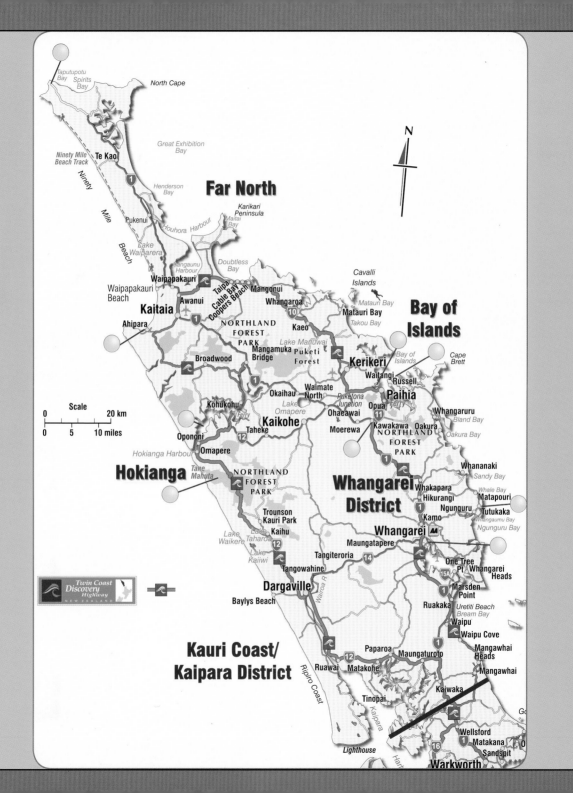

Ahipara: Sacred Fire

Perhaps you've arrived in Kaitaia at the apex of your Twin Coast Discovery Highway tour, or perhaps you're travelling to Cape Reinga. Quite frankly, you'd be mad if you didn't make the 20-minute detour to Ahipara out on the west coast.

The little settlement of Ahipara is at the southern extremity of the matchless Ninety Mile Beach. Ahipara means 'sacred fire'. The name was bestowed by the Te Rarawa people, whose ancestral waka, Tinana, made landfall here.

After European settlement, Ahipara was home to some 2000 people at the height of the industry that sprang up about kauri gum as an export commodity. When

Shipwreck Bay, Ahipara, forms the southern end of Ninety Mile Beach.

JANET LEWIS

worldwide demand for kauri gum tailed off in the 1950s, Ahipara became one of Northland's best-kept secrets, known only to the few beachcombers who maintained picturesque, ramshackle baches here and, of course, to the surfing community. Lately, stylish, modern housing is beginning to jostle with those old baches overlooking the Tasman Sea. The secret is getting out.

Southwest of the settlement, and beneath the towering sand-dunes of the Tauroa Peninsula, is Shipwreck Bay. A world-class surf break, it receives a great, rolling swell from the Tasman that peels along Reef Point and polishes up beautifully whenever the wind blows from the southerly quarter.

Shipwreck Bay's name is a mournful memento of the many wrecks that have occurred along this stretch of coastline, as vessels caught on this long, inhospitable lee shore sought the minimal shelter of the bay, only to be driven ashore by wild westerlies. The remains of one wreck, the *Favourite*, can still be seen at low tide.

You'll probably want to stick around in Ahipara. Accommodation ranges from a campground to several bed-and-breakfast establishments, and some bach owners are willing to rent their slice of paradise, too. There's a heap to do here: swimming and surfing, of course, and foraging for kai moana — especially delicately flavoured tuatua in the shallows — but there's also quad biking, surfcasting, horse riding and land yachting. You can also explore the Ahipara Gumfields Scenic Reserve, where the remnants of the workings will give

you some idea of the hardships endured by those doughty pioneers. You can do this on foot, or by tagging along on a guided quad-bike tour. Or, of course, you can simply sit back on the deck in the evening and contemplate the splendours of the sunset — sacred fire indeed.

I LOVE YOU NEW ZEALAND

Stay in either of the two end units at the Ahipara Bay Motel with some of the very best views and best sunsets anywhere in New Zealand. Excellent food in the licensed restaurant too. Plus Neil and Raewyn's hospitality is great! And if you surf, when this place is on, it is probably the best or second best break in the country!
Barron Braden

The 102s

Karikari Peninsula is the closest thing to heaven you will find in Northland. From the white-sand beaches at Rangiputa around to the amazing swimming beach at Maitai Bay, which is very safe to swim and snorkel in. There is a camp site next to the beach and it is very secluded and safe. It is fully utilised during the summer season by a mixture of Kiwis and tourists in their campervans or mobile homes.
David Coleman

Bay of Islands

Captain James Cook had some moments of inspiration when he was floating about naming bits of New Zealand. It's fair to say the Bay of Islands is not his best work. It is, as the name doggedly suggests, a bay featuring nearly 150 islands of various sizes, formed when rising sea levels drowned a maze of river valleys.

Visiting the Hole in the Rock at Piercy Island is the quintessential Bay of Islands experience.

What its name lacks in imagination, however, it more than makes up for in attractions. It is, quite simply, one of the world's greatest cruising locations.

You can sample some of its charms from the land. The towns of Paihia and

The tourist hub of Paihia, Bay of Islands.

Russell are popular destinations for summer holidays, and for those who are disposed to look a little more deeply, the area is rich in historical interest. Being a kind of kai moana central, with a climate approximating the chillier bits of Polynesia, it was a densely settled area in Maori times. It was also the site of the earliest permanent European settlements. Indeed, Russell had the distinction of being New Zealand's first capital — until everyone realised it was far too nice to spoil by populating it with politicians.

To really appreciate the Bay of Islands, you've got to hop aboard a boat. Happily for those who don't own a yacht, there are plenty of options that don't involve piracy or stowing away. Daily cruises take visitors on a tour to the larger islands and out to Piercy Island, where in favourable sea conditions, you can cruise through the famed Hole in the Rock. Other excursions will get you up close and personal with the area's resident dolphins, take you to the

countless diving spots (even if it's just the cool snorkelling lagoon on Roberton Island) or aid and abet you in your efforts to hook one of the many marlin or snapper that abound in these waters.

There are charter vessels available, too, ranging from kayaks, dinghies and catamarans to trailer-sailers, fizzboats and luxury yachts and launches. In the end, if you haven't sat, cool drink in hand, and watched the sun set from the deck of a boat at anchor in Moturua Island's Goodfellows Bay of a summer evening, you haven't lived. It's as simple as that.

FAVOURITES

BEST ICE CREAM
Bay of Islands Ice Cream Company, 84 Kerikeri Rd, Kerikeri

BEST FRESH STUFF
Bay of Islands Farmers' Market in Hobson Ave, KeriKeri

BEST TRIP FOR FOODIES
Northland Food and Wine Trail

BEST SEAFOOD
The Sugar Boat, Waitangi Bridge, Paihia

BEST VINO
Omata Estate Vineyard Restaurant, Aucks Rd, Russell

DESTINATION NORTHLAND

Roberton Island, one of the jewels of the Bay of Islands.

Cape Reinga

As you climb the high, lonely road that eventually winds down to Cape Reinga the land narrows, affording glimpses of Northland's east and west coasts. Once you're there, there's only ocean in front of you, the currents of the Pacific and the Tasman, which the North Island has for so long kept apart, enjoying a wild and turbulent reunion.

Even on a rare calm day, a cool breeze tickles your spine as you contemplate the final meeting of land and water, with the whisper of those two battling oceans rising to your ears.

It's easy to see how the Maori came to revere this place, for how could you stand here and not feel a twinge of yearning for the remembered homeland, across the ocean? As you stand at the lighthouse, the land hunches its shoulders in a last hump below and to the right — Cape Reinga

itself. Clinging to the eastern side of the headland is an 800-year-old pohutukawa, known to the Maori as Te Rerenga Wairua, 'the leaping place of spirits'. Here, according to legend, the spirits of the deceased end the land-bound part of the journey back to Hawaiki, the land of the ancestors. After leaping into the green water beneath the tree, spirits would make their way northward underwater, pausing for one last, regretful look back before plunging forever into the underworld.

To the west of the cape, the taut white arc of Te Werahi Beach stretches to Cape Maria van Diemen, named by Abel Tasman for his patron's daughter. To the east, beyond the closer headlands, you can see the eastern extremity of Spirits Bay and, farther yet, the Surville Cliffs, the northernmost point of the New Zealand mainland.

The lighthouse at Cape Reinga.

The seemingly endless stretch of Ninety Mile Beach.

JANET LEWIS

DESTINATION NORTHLAND

101 MUST-DO'S FOR KIWIS **AA**

Approaching or leaving Cape Reinga, you would do well to visit Te Paki Stream, where dunes of white sand of Saharan proportions rear at the northern end of Ninety Mile Beach. Careful where you stop: local lore has it that Te Paki has tracts of quicksand that can swallow an SUV whole.

Rental car companies forbid you to take their vehicles onto Ninety Mile Beach itself, but a drive along the beach — closer to 90 kilometres in length, despite the name — is one of those things every New Zealander must experience at least once.

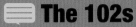

The 102s

The beautiful and unique fiord-like **Whangaroa Harbour** in the Far North. Sail around and view the magnificent rock formations then cruise out to the uninhabited Cavalli Islands: blue penguins, dolphins, maybe orca, birdlife, clear water, white sand — **magic!** Lee Brogan

I LOVE YOU NEW ZEALAND

Absolutely loved the trip to Cape Reinga with a wonderful bus driver who got my daughter (who has Down Syndrome) to slide down the sand dunes on a boogie board.
Sandra Boock

Wherever you're from the signpost at Cape Reinga will give you a good indication of how far from home you really are . . .

The headland at Cape Reinga.

JANET LEWIS

JANET LEWIS

Hokianga

DESTINATION NORTHLAND

Giant sand-dunes mark the entrance to the Hokianga Harbour.

The Hokianga Harbour (which means 'the returning') is named in commemoration of the legendary Polynesian navigator, Kupe, who ended his exploration of New Zealand here and departed for Hawaiki. But it could just as easily refer to the vow you make on every occasion you spend time here, because it's a place that just keeps drawing you back.

The most rewarding direction in which to approach the Hokianga is from the south along State Highway 12, which is also the leg of the Twin Coast Discovery Highway route that features the great Waipoua and Trounson kauri forests (see page 20).

About half an hour after you leave Waipoua Forest, you come over a hill and there's the long, turquoise Hokianga stretched out below you, with the dazzling sand dunes of the northern headland ahead. You drop down to the popular holiday destination of Omapere and you're there in the Hokianga proper.

The southern shore has plenty to offer the visitor. There's campgrounds at Omapere, Opononi and Rawene, cafés and craft shops in Rawene, a number of the oldest churches in the country, Rawene's Clendon House (the residence of early settler, trader and some-time US Consul to New Zealand, James Reddy Clendon) and a Hinuera stone statue of Opo the dolphin outside the famous Opononi pub. Opo was a female bottlenose dolphin who delighted New Zealanders by apparently seeking out and enjoying human contact in the shallows off Opononi in the summer of 1955–6.

A short drive out to the lookout point on the harbour's South Head is rewarded with spectacular views of the turbulent sandbar at the entrance to the harbour and the opposite headland's dunes. If you find the latter just too enticing, you can either take a water taxi from Opononi and land on North Head directly, or drive, taking the regular vehicular ferry service between Rawene and Kohukohu, a former timber town on the northern shore.

It's a struggle to the top of the dunes, especially in high summer, where the fine white sand reflects the blazing sun full blast, but it's rewarding. A handful of giant strides will get you down in seconds from the heights it takes you ten minutes to scale. Better yet, if you took the precaution of equipping yourself with a plastic surfboard, you can toboggan down at breakneck speed. Recommended for kids aged five to 105.

I LOVE YOU NEW ZEALAND

Unspoilt beauty. Only thing you should take is your photos and the only thing to leave are your footprints. Raewyn Smythe

Clendon House — a stirring story of early New Zealand and the people who made Hokianga their home sweet home. Lindsay Charman

The 102s

Soda Springs, on the climb into the Mangamukas from the south. A hidden magical swimming hole, and a must for travellers with children who need to cool off, before the last stomach-defying ascent of the range before Kaitaia . . . Look for the small sign on the left on State Highway 12, about five kilometres from Mangamuka. Nicola Smith

There are plenty of craft shops to explore in the Hokianga.

Hundertwasser Toilets

Friedensreich Hundertwasser was born in Austria and already had an international reputation as an artist when he first visited New Zealand in 1973 accompanying a major exhibition of his works that was touring the country. He liked the place so much that he bought a little slice of paradise on the Waikino Peninsula in the Bay of Islands. His intention was to divide his time between Europe and New Zealand, but he soon made the only truly rational choice: he became a New Zealand citizen in 1983, and gifted the nation a new flag — featuring a bold, green koru motif — as a kind of *quid pro quo*.

Waikino where he made his home translates as 'bad water' but by 1998, any bad water lying about there had nothing on the 40-year-old public dunny in nearby Kawakawa. This had become just another powerful incentive for tourists to bypass the burnt-out coal-mining town. The community board decided something had to be done about it and they consulted Hundertwasser.

Using an eclectic assortment of materials, including bricks recycled from the recently demolished Bank of New Zealand building, tiles made by students at Bay of Islands College, empty bottles, concrete, steel, copper and bits and pieces of ceramics from his own studio, the Austrian maestro constructed the new Kawakawa conveniences around a tree.

The new loos became an overnight celebrity, receiving an award from Creative New Zealand and another for landscape design. Foreign television crews showed up — presumably much to the discomfort of those using the loo at the time — and soon the Hundertwasser toilets became one of New Zealand's most photographed attractions.

As the great artist died in 2000, the Kawakawa toilets will remain the only Hundertwasser-designed structure in the southern hemisphere (although other little, brilliantly coloured, eccentrically devised objects about town bear the unmistakeable Hundertwasser touch).

Picasso has his *Guernica*. Da Vinci has his *Mona Lisa*. Michaelangelo has his *David*. Hundertwasser has his dunny.

I LOVE YOU NEW ZEALAND

Only in New Zealand! Very artsy and there's a gallery over the road that specialises in Hunterwasser prints, etc. Francie Besson

I've never been so keen to go to a public toilet! Worth a look even if you don't need to pee! Cheryll Butters

DESTINATION NORTHLAND

Make a comfort stop at the Hundertwasser Toilets, Kawakawa.

17

Tutukaka/The Poor Knights

We are a maritime nation. New Zealand is blessed with ample coastline and most of us find some way of enjoying ourselves in, around and under the water.

One of the best destinations for those who want to experience the full range of watery pastimes is the east coast of Northland, and in particular Tutukaka, just to the northeast of Whangarei.

This little settlement really jumps in the summer. It's a natural waypoint for yachts en route up and down the coast and holiday-making landlubbers alike. Just north of Tutukaka, Matapouri Bay marks the start of a chain of superb white-sand beaches that scallop the coastline north to the Bay of Islands and beyond.

Tutukaka is also the hub of an extensive network of fishing and diving charters. Game-fish species abound in the deep blue Pacific water that washes this coast: at Tutukaka, you can hook up with a boat running everything from day charters to longer excursions as far north as the Three Kings Islands.

Tutukaka is also the gateway to the major diving spots of the Northland coast — the 'Twin Wrecks', two ex-navy vessels sunk to provide diving wrecks, and, of course, the Poor Knights Islands.

Many dive spots around our coastline have their advocates in the stakes for the best in the country. But most divers will agree that the Poor Knights are unrivalled, with the happy coincidence of their proximity to the continental shelf, the

Charter boats head for the Poor Knights Islands from the Tutukaka Marina.

DESTINATION NORTHLAND

influence of a warm ocean current and the unusually good visibility that is present year-round — not to mention the sheer variety of the terrain.

There are over 50 notable scuba-diving spots around the islands, named by pioneering divers and charter boat operators over the years, which cater to snorkellers and the novice scuba diver (Nursery Cove, for example) and to more advanced divers (such as the adrenaline-pumping Wild Beast Point). In between, there are archways, drop-offs, canyons, kelp forests and the giant, acoustically fantastic Rikoriko sea-cave (allegedly the largest in the world), which is nearly as interesting to visit on the surface as underwater.

Every known northern species of fish is not only present but thrives and some species properly distributed in the waters far to the north of New Zealand are encountered here too. Such was the obvious uniqueness of the area that for years, the Knights enjoyed a voluntary but almost universally observed spear-fishing ban among divers and the islands were sensitively treated by line fishermen. In 1981, they were made New Zealand's second marine reserve.

They're a national treasure, and they're just waiting for you to take the plunge.

The 102s

Whangarei Quarry Gardens, a tropical garden hewn out of an old quarry site in the centre of Whangarei. The determination of many volunteers has overcome many obstacles to convert what could have remained a weed-covered eyesore into a place of beauty and tranquillity. Carole Brackenbury

Close encounter with a stingray, Poor Knights Islands.

DESTINATION NORTHLAND

I LOVE YOU NEW ZEALAND

Middle earth in the middle of the ocean. Kate Malcolm

Waipoua Forest

Kauri forest once covered over 1.2 million hectares of the North Island, from the mid-Waikato northward. Trouble was, it was such beautiful woodworking timber that much of our mighty forest was quickly turned into spars for British warships or consumed by the Victorian residential housing boom.

As a consequence, there are only sad remnants of the majestic kauri forest left, and only glimpses may be had today of what our country would have looked like before the coming of the axe and the crosscut saw.

Two areas in Northland where you can get a sense of this are on the Kauri Coast leg of the Twin Coast Discovery Highway touring route.

The first you come to driving north is Trounson Kauri Park at Aronga, near Dargaville, where you can see and learn about the ecology of the kauri forest, including some of the shy critters that live there — fearsome-looking wetas, the kauri snail and the North Island brown kiwi. At nearby Matakohe, there's the Kauri Museum, which has displays telling the story of the exploitation of kauri — the timber and the gum industries that were for a while the mainstay of the Northland economy.

Further north, there's Waipoua Forest, internationally famous as the most representative remnant of the great kauri forests of pre-European times. We're pretty lucky to have it. When the government was finally prevailed upon in 1952 to set aside a forest sanctuary of 90,000-odd hectares, the axemen and sawyers were already eyeing it and sharpening their blades.

A short walk off the road along a track and boardwalks — essential to protect the

Explore the native bush at Waipoua Forest.

DESTINATION NORTHLAND

delicate roots of kauri from the trampling feet of visitors — is the awe-inspiring Tane Mahuta, the largest kauri tree remaining in the world. It is the highlight of a visit to Waipoua. At 17.88 metres from the ground to the first branch, with the tips of the uppermost branches waving in the breeze at 51.5 metres overhead, it's pretty big! But the truly impressive aspect of the Lord of the Forest is his girth: his pale bole measures a massive 13.77 metres around.

The statistics can't prepare you for the sight, nor can photographs. It isn't easy to get your head around the fact that this tree has witnessed the entire human history of Aotearoa/New Zealand, and was already a mature tree when Christ was a lad.

You'll go away determined to plant a kauri, and to be very careful about where you plant it.

📃 The 102s

Pahi on the Northern Kaipara — a gem. Nearby is the site of Jane Mander's *Story of a New Zealand River* and in the other direction the Matakohe Kauri Museum. For the more action minded go inland for the Rally of New Zealand on the Possum-Bull Run or the Waipu Gorge, or just experience the back country peace and quiet. This is such a great country, who would want to go overseas. John Paynter

'Lord of the Forest', Tane Mahuta, Waipoua Forest.

DESTINATION NORTHLAND

Waitangi Treaty Grounds

The Treaty of Waitangi is a strange sort of document. It was cobbled together in haste by William Hobson, the young naval officer dispatched from New South Wales to take matters in hand, tinkered with by the resident British magistrate, James Busby, and then loosely translated into Maori by missionary Henry Williams and his son, Edward. It was presented to a large gathering of Maori chiefs on the lawn of Busby's house, the Residency, at Waitangi on Wednesday, 5 February 1840. After a brisk debate, the treaty was signed by most of those present the following day.

In presenting the treaty, the British expected to take complete control of Aotearoa/New Zealand and all who lived there, assuming in particular the right to regulate the sale and purchase of land. In signing, most Maori believed they were receiving protection from the British Crown from the depredations of 'the French or the rum sellers'.

It was the beginning of New Zealand as a nation: what a pity it had to be based on a misunderstanding. Nonetheless, the two peoples were now united, for better or worse, in something resembling holy matrimony and, like most marriages, there would be rough patches and smooth.

Interest in the treaty among New Zealanders of European descent began to revive after a long period of oblivion when James Busby's decaying Residency was gifted to the people of New Zealand by the then Governor-General, Lord Bledisloe, in 1932. The Treaty House, as it became known, was restored as a 'national memorial' — a memento of the signing of the treaty — and so it has remained. A carved wharenui was subsequently erected alongside to symbolise the partnership between the peoples.

Every year, representatives of both parties to the treaty gather at nearby Te Tii marae to reaffirm their commitment to the union. The occasion is seldom free from friction, but at least everyone is still talking.

Waitangi Day, 6 February, is the best time to visit, but the Treaty House is open year round, and guided tours are available. A cultural group, He Tohu, performs a fiery haka several times a day, and the visitor centre runs audio-visual displays illuminating the events of 1840 and the course of the Maori-Pakeha relationship ever since. There's an artefacts room, where treaty-related taonga are displayed. A waka taua — a ceremonial war canoe — is on display in the grounds, and on the manicured lawns out front, there's a flagstaff erected where the treaty was first signed all those years ago.

Under that flagstaff is the perfect place to contemplate the Bay of Islands, and to reflect on how far we've all come, side by side.

The grounds of
the Waitangi
Treaty House
overlook the
Bay of Islands.

101 MUST-DO'S
FOR KIWIS

Auckland

Few of the world's great cities can boast a location like Auckland's. It has the Hauraki Gulf at its front door, and the wild west coast beaches at its back. The region has countless attractions and activities. And it's all built on a volcanic field that could go up at any moment . . .

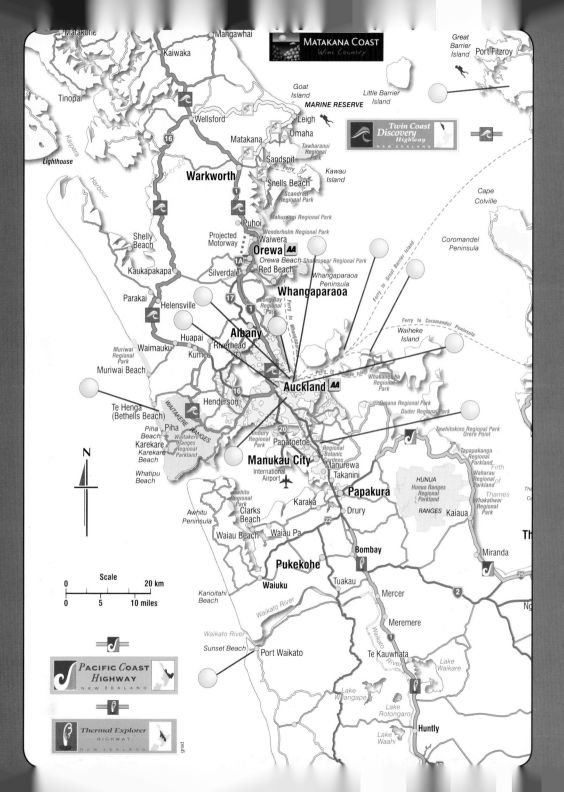

Animal Crazy

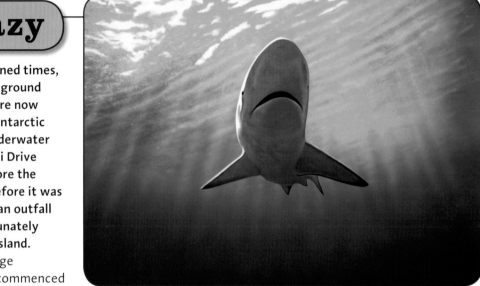

In less enlightened times, the vast underground chambers that are now Kelly Tarlton's Antarctic Encounter & Underwater World on Tamaki Drive were used to store the city's sewage before it was pumped raw to an outfall near the unfortunately named Browns Island.

Once sewerage treatment was commenced elsewhere, however, the tanks lay idle. It took the vision of scuba-diving legend, Kelly Tarlton, to see them transformed into an internationally renowned tourist attraction — destiny in motions.

Tarlton's idea was to put something of the world he knew from his underwater adventures in front of people who were afraid to get their feet wet, let alone abandon their natural habitat and mix with the fishes.

He designed a 110-metre long series of transparent tunnels through the tanks, which he proposed to fill with a faithful recreation of the marine environment, complete with millions of litres of seawater and a cross-section of the critters that call the sea home. It hadn't been done before, but Tarlton and his team just went ahead and made it happen.

A basic tour of Kelly Tarlton's

Keep a safe distance or swim with a bronze whaler shark at Kelly Tarlton's.

See the penguins on an Antarctic Encounter at Kelly Tarlton's.

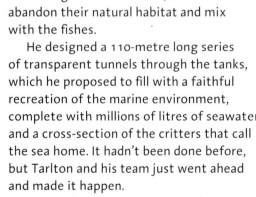

is fascinating enough. You can cruise along the walkways and lock eyes with everything from urchins and octopi to stingrays, sharks and that little fish with the big reputation, the piranha.

You can do the Antarctic Encounter tour, entering through a replica of Sir Robert Falcon Scott's hut, boarding a Snow Cat (such as are used on the ice) for a ride past the resident penguin colony, as they cool their heels in the three tonnes of fresh snow that's made daily just for them.

But if you bring your togs along, there are more interactive tours you can join. Stingray Splash puts you in the water with these graceful creatures, as close as you're likely to want to get in these post-Steve Irwin days. No diving or snorkelling experience is needed. In Shark Survival,

they'll kit you up in full scuba gear and put you in the water at feeding time so you can see these beautiful creatures up close and personal. Again, no previous scuba experience is necessary.

If you've acquired a taste for close encounters with animals, then you can further indulge it at Auckland Zoo, where a ZOOM pass will let you experience first-hand what it's like to help a keeper wash down an elephant, hand-feed the Madagascan ring-tailed lemurs and South American cotton-topped tamarins, or head into the cheetah's enclosure to feel the V8 rumble of a purring big cat through its velvety coat.

I LOVE YOU NEW ZEALAND

Big kids go along with a bit of trepidation — will we love or hate it! Have no fear, it's as good for us as it is for the littlies (probably even better!!) Andrea Youngs

AUCKLAND ZOO

Hand feed one of these little fellas at the zoo.

Auckland War Memorial Museum

The museum tells the story of New Zealand, its place in the Pacific and its people.

Our children will have completely different memories of the Auckland War Memorial Museum than the majority of us have borne from our past.

Forget the moth-eaten, sad-eyed elephant, reeking of embalming fluid. Forget the dark, creepy Victorian village. Our kids will remember their nocturnal dinosaur hunt (if they were lucky enough to catch the *Dinos after Dark* exhibit), the fantastic sight of the Auckland volcanic field in full eruption, or something else to equal these, given the museum's exciting programme of interactive exhibits.

They will find plenty to do and remember in the Stevenson Discovery Centres, featuring the *Weird and the Wonderful*, and the *Treasure and Tales* exhibits. The brand new Storyspace facility will bring aspects of New Zealand's past and the museum's collections alive for kids.

The first Auckland Museum began in a disused government farm building on the corner of Symonds Street and Grafton Road in 1852, housing the collections of amateur enthusiasts and naturalists. It's grown like topsy since then. In 1920, the city fathers decided to construct and consecrate the present, magnificent neoclassical building — the museum's fifth home — to the memory of those who fell in the First World War. A competition was held and the winning design by Auckland firm Grierson, Aimer and Draffin was chosen from an international field of entries. The chosen site was a spot in the Auckland Domain — actually the eroded cone of an extinct volcano — called Observation Hill, giving commanding views of the Waitemata Harbour and the growing city. Once construction was complete, the collections shifted to their new premises and the Museum reopened to the public in 1929. It was extended in 1960, with a great curved chamber engraved with the names of the Glorious Dead constructed to the rear of the original building. A major renovation — including the fitting of a huge revolving door — was completed in 1999, and the building

Auckland War Memorial Museum and The Dome.

has recently been expanded again, with the rear courtyard converted into a breathtaking new space known as The Dome — a vast copper and glass dome that was opened in December 2006.

The permanent collection houses some 2.7 million items, including the largest array of Maori taonga in the world and a leading natural history collection.

The museum regularly features internationally acclaimed visiting displays. The emphasis is now firmly on the interactive rather than the dead and the passive, a far cry from the museums of the past.

It's an Auckland icon, a treasure house and a national treasure in its own right.

Marvel at cultures from around the world in the *Treasures and Tales* exhibit at the Stevenson Discovery Centre.

AUCKLAND WAR MEMORIAL MUSEUM

Auckland's Islands

Auckland is known as the City of Sails, largely because it has some of the world's best cruising waters on its doorstep. The Hauraki Gulf is an unparalleled marine playground, studded with over 50 islands, each with its own natural and historical features to discover and explore.

Rangitoto Island is an icon of Auckland, and many Aucklanders have not made the pilgrimage across the shipping channel by ferry, private boat or sea kayak to admire the gulf from its 259 metre summit. Some once kept baches near the ferry landing at Islington Bay, and many of these baches survive, nestled on the rocky shoreline among the regenerating bush, which includes the world's largest pohutukawa forest.

Rangitoto Island is an icon of Auckland.

Take a stroll around Stonyridge Vineyard on Waiheke Island before indulging in a glass of red.

Across a causeway from the ferry wharf is Motutapu Island, and just across the channel — a few minutes longer on the ferry — is Motuihe Island, once the site of a children's health camp and now a popular picnic destination.

Beyond the gateway formed by Motutapu and Motuihe is the long, low outline of Waiheke Island, which nowadays is a cross between an Auckland suburb — albeit a somewhat bohemian one — and a holiday resort. Vineyards, olive groves, cafés, restaurants and art galleries sit alongside its stunning ocean beaches, making Waiheke a treat for day-trippers and holiday-makers alike.

Tiritiri Matangi Island, a one-hour ferry ride from downtown Auckland, has become an internationally recognised conservation success story. It has been cleared of introduced predators and planted with more than 300,000 native trees. Visitors can see and interact with 11 threatened native bird species (including the extremely rare

PHAEDRA CADNESS

PHAEDRA CADNESS

takahe) and the tuatara.

Kawau Island is among the most popular destinations for Auckland's vast pleasure boat fleet. It boasts excellent anchorages and a wealth of locations of historical interest, including the collection of exotic flora and fauna with which Governor George Grey surrounded his gracious home in Mansion House Bay.

A visit to Great Barrier Island is like stepping back to the New Zealand of 20 years ago. The hinterland of the two main settlements at Port Fitzroy and Tryphena is rugged and beautiful, with some of the region's best beaches and more than 100 kilometres of well-maintained tracks for trampers. The view from the island's highest point, the 627 metre Mount Hobson, is not won without a certain amount of struggle, but it's magic — all the islands of the gulf scattered jewel-like between you and Auckland's Sky Tower, 90 kilometres distant as the kereru flies.

The 102s

Being part of the crew as you sail on Sir Peter Blake's Lion New Zealand yacht which competed in the Whitbread Round the World Race. Sailing 120 nautical miles from Auckland up to the Bay of Islands experiencing not only being one with all the elements that offshore sailing throws at you, but surrounded by dolphins, flying fish and blue penguins. Also the thrill, romance and emotional sensation of following in the footsteps of New Zealand's greatest sailor.
Hilary Bull

PHAEDRA CADNESS

The view from the top of Mount Hobson on Great Barrier Island is worth the struggle.

Auckland's Volcanoes

You might think it says something about our opinion of politicians that New Zealand's capital city, Wellington, is situated on an active fault line — especially when you remember that the previous capital is located smack bang on a volcanic field.

The youngest of Auckland's volcanic vents is Rangitoto Island, which last blew its top about 800 years ago — just yesterday in geological terms — but all in all there are over 60 sites of bygone volcanic activity scattered about the Auckland isthmus.

Many of these are pretty obvious. Before the Sky Tower came along, Mount Eden and One Tree Hill used to be the city's prime panoramic vantage points. Well, they're still there, and they're free. The dayshift on both summits sees Aucklanders and tour operators pointing out the sights to visitors, while after dark, teenagers take time out from snogging to admire all the pretty lights below.

Mount Eden — Maungawhau in Maori — is the tallest of Auckland's surviving volcanic cones. Its former rivals find themselves in reduced circumstances, many having been quarried to supply the field-drain and scoria-wall appetites of Auckland's landscapers down through time.

Today's visitors puzzle over the European name of Maungakiekie, One Tree Hill, which is the focal point of the lovely Cornwall Park. It was named for a prominent totara tree that used to grow there in the early days of European settlement. Later generations of Aucklanders identified with the lone Monterey pine that leaned elegantly toward the obelisk commemorating city father, Sir John Logan Campbell. The tree was removed in 2000, having been mortally wounded by a chainsaw-wielding protestor. The Tree part of One Tree Hill is presently a restoration work in progress.

Both Maungawhau and Maungakiekie are points of note along Auckland's coast-to-coast walking route. Like many of the city's volcanic cones, they are rich in geological and historical interest, with the distinctive terracing of Maori fortification still clearly visible on their flanks.

Across the harbour, there's North Head and Mount Victoria, which each have their own talking points. North Head is a natural vantage point from which to watch the comings and goings on the Waitemata Harbour, and that's why the martial minds of Maori and Pakeha alike selected it for fortification. Out in the gulf, there's pretty little Motukorea/Browns Island (so named by Maori after the local population of oystercatchers) and of course, Rangitoto.

All's quiet in the Auckland volcanic field these days, but they're tricky customers these volcanoes. You never know when they're going to cut up rough. Perhaps you'd better get in and visit while the going's good.

The view from the top of Mount Eden at sunset is awe-inspiring.

101 MUST-DO'S FOR KIWIS

Auckland's West Coast

Say what you like about Auckland and its residents, you've got to admit that both are blessed with the region's beaches. They're within an hour's drive of the kind of sand and surf action that others, less fortunate than themselves, would love to have.

Sure, there's the pleasant, placid, white-sand beaches of the east coast, but for the genuine coastal connoisseur, the real action is out west. From the secluded beach at Whatipu, north of the entrance to the Manukau Harbour, north to Rangitira Beach at the southern entrance to the Kaipara Harbour, the west coast beaches are strung like black pearls.

The Waitakere Ranges were formed by volcanic activity over a period of 22 million years. The volcanic rock has weathered and washed in to the sea, depositing a fine purple-black sand rich in iron oxide. Feeling your feet sizzle in the superheated sand of Bethells/Te Henga, Piha or Muriwai is one of Auckland's quintessential summer experiences.

They may lack the conventional good looks of the white-sand beauties back east, but these beaches are movie stars. Moody Karekare starred in Jane Campion's film, *The Piano*. Up the line, Bethells/Te Henga served as a backdrop for *Xena: Warrior Princess* and *Hercules: The Legendary Journeys*.

In any weather, the solemn, cathedral-like coves of Bethells/Te Henga, Piha and Karekare do atmosphere

I LOVE YOU NEW ZEALAND

Whatipu is so rugged and raw. I love the landscape and the wildness of the place. It will always hold a special place in my heart, because that's where my partner proposed to me! I said 'yes' of course! Ceilla Govind

I live west of Auckland (and have all my life — yeah I'm a westie!) I've experienced most of the beaches along the west coast ... so many memories: the huge waves at Piha, the people we've met at the beaches over the years, the laughs, and the feeds — fish and chips!!
Lelia Bourne

hugely well. Even on a fine day, when an easterly has polished the swell into glassy barrels, there's a sense of muscularity about the Tasman Sea's attention to the rocky coastline, and an intimacy created by the dense rainforest that crowds the dunes. Of course, when the weather cuts up rough, you can't beat Piha or Muriwai for a show of raw, oceanic power. Swimmers, surfers and fishermen love and fear this coast in equal measure.

The 60 kilometre beach at Muriwai is a registered public road, and is a popular destination for weekend cowboys seeking sand and cred to stick to the fenders of their four-wheel-drives. It's also a peerless place to gallop a hired horse. At its southern end, you can visit one of New Zealand's only mainland gannet colonies. Or you can just spread the rug out and savour the uniquely west coast taste sensation that is ironsand in your sandwiches.

Lion Rock at Piha Beach is a commanding presence.

Devonport and North Head

PHOTO NEW ZEALAND

The local iwi, Ngati Whatua, were the first to scope Takapuna, Takarunga and Takaroro — the three volcanic cones at the end of the northern headland of Auckland's Waitemata Harbour — as ideal defensive positions. The biggest and strongest of the pa they built was atop the seaward of the three, which they named Maunga Uika. The terraces of their fortifications can still be seen today.

When the Europeans arrived, they too saw the strategic potential of the headland. Not long after Devonport — named Flagstaff until it assumed its present, Anglophile name in 1859 — was founded, a naval base was sited on Mount Victoria (the renamed Takarunga), complete with dockyards below in Stanley Bay.

At the end of the nineteenth century, Maunga Uika (now known by the unimaginative name of North Head) was fortified all over again. This time, the hill was riven with a honeycomb of tunnels housing bunkers, barracks, magazines and gun emplacements. The Russians were coming, you see, and our defensive master-plan was to arm North Head to the teeth so that when the Russian armada appeared in the Rangitoto Channel (as they certainly must), we could blow it out of the water and win a famous victory for the greater glory of the British Empire . . .

Well, it all made sense at the time. Today, you can still see and even explore some of the tunnels, and the main emplacement still houses an 8-inch Armstrong 'disappearing' gun. This was mechanically contrived to pop up out of its hole to lob a shell at the unwary Russians and drop back out of sight before they could splutter 'Where the hellski did that come from?'

Take the ferry to Devonport and leave the city behind.

Just as entertaining as late Victorian military strategy, contemporary theory holds that the lion's share of the original tunnels are still there, sealed off and disguised, and packed with all manner of military secret stuff, from frighteningly unstable First World War ordnance to a couple of Boeing seaplanes used by Auckland's Walsh Brothers for their once-famous flying school.

Who knows? Whatever the truth, with its splendid views of the Hauraki Gulf, North Head is the logical location for a picnic day out, which can also include lazing nearby on some of Auckland's prettiest beaches, and exploring the shops and cafés in Devonport's main street. Or you could catch a ferry across from Auckland City — as Aucklanders have been doing for as long as there have been Aucklanders — to enjoy a night out at one of Devonport's many restaurants and bars.

Devonport is so nice, it's no wonder the locals want to secede. And they've got the best defensive position in town.

The 102s

For Auckland, an awesome free day out is swimming and relaxing on beautiful Cheltenham Beach looking out to Rangitoto Island. Then walk along the beach and up the steps to North Head. Take a torch and explore the old naval ruins and a piece of cardboard for an adrenalin ride down the grassy slopes.
Janet Board

FAVOURITES

BEST CHILL
Head to Cheltenham Beach with a picnic

BEST SECONDHAND READ
Evergreen Books, 15 Victoria Rd

BEST COFFEE
Zigana Café, 46 Victoria Rd

BEST BREAD
Devonport Stone Oven Bakery and Café, 5 Clarence St

PHOTO NEW ZEALAND

Looking towards the city from North Head.

Skyjump and Sky Tower

Anyone who's ever brewed up a mix in a wheelbarrow will be interested to know it took 28,000 tonnes of concrete to build Auckland's Sky Tower. Opening in 1997, it was, at 326 metres above sea level, the tallest building in the southern hemisphere. It's still the twelfth tallest tower in the world, and stands there proudly, a testimony to the Kiwi desire to find the tallest thing in the area and jump off it.

If you asked any one of the gamblers entering the grand glass doors of the Skycity Casino in central Auckland what they reckoned your chances were of surviving if you jumped off the Sky Tower, 192 metres above the concrete, you could be pretty sure they'd lay long odds.

Aha! But there's a set of gizmoes installed way up there to let you do precisely that.

First, they'll strap you into a jump suit. Then they'll clip you onto one end of a cable that's wrapped around a winch and run a few reassuring checks. Then they'll show you the door, beyond which lies nearly 200 metres of airy void.

Whereas under uncontrolled conditions it'd be a matter of moments before you hit the ground, it wouldn't make for much of a tourism venture. Punters wouldn't have time to enjoy it, the nice people at Skycity would be forever cleaning up the footpath and there'd be a distinct lack of return custom.

What they've contrived in the

I LOVE YOU NEW ZEALAND

Skyjump is the quickest way down from the Sky Tower — beats the lifts every time! Brent O'Hagan

Skyjump is to delay the inevitable — slow you down to a maximum speed of 75 km/h and bring you to a gentle halt before the earth does. This way, you spend 16 seconds in transit: time enough to get over your blind terror and enjoy the view.

And what a view! Even the hardened hearts of those who opposed the Sky Tower concept back in the early 1990s have been won over by the vista from the top. Not even Mount Eden can deliver the kind of panorama available from the observation deck, 220 metres above pavement level.

The lights of Auckland and the gulf make for chic wallpaper. If high-altitude dining is your thing, The Observatory, one deck down from the observation deck, offers brasserie-style buffet fare. Or there's Orbit, which offers an à la carte menu showcasing superb New Zealand cuisine, even as the room rotates around you. And nope, it's nothing to do with the wine . . .

Auckland Sky Tower looms high over Auckland city and the Waitemata Harbour — would you jump off it?

101 MUST-DO'S
FOR KIWIS

Franklin & Waikato

The Tasman Sea interacts with New Zealand's west coast pretty vigorously, and in those spots where the sea floor and landforms are just right, all that energy is transformed into hollow-hearted, glassy surf. Raglan and Port Waikato are two such places — and you should see the sunsets.

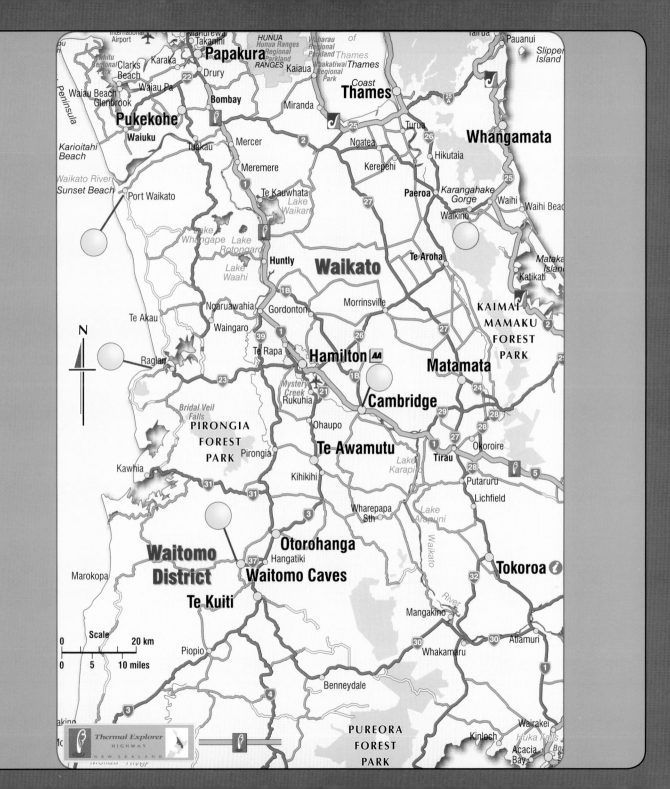

Port Waikato

Those unfamiliar with New Zealand geography are often surprised to find the Waikato River, which they first meet at Taupo in the heart of the Central Plateau, cropping up again and again as they drive north. And if they happen to head out west just south of Auckland, they're further surprised to find the Waikato emptying into the Tasman right there, after its 425 kilometre journey.

The river terminates in a swampy delta, an estuary and then a shallow bar harbour, once maintained as a sea port. The area is still called Port Waikato, commemorating the coastal trade that passed this way, the naval expeditions that departed upriver to harass the Maori in the 1860s and the occasional shipment of sand and shingle that still heads north to the Manukau Harbour from here.

The main drawcard of Port Waikato is no longer commerce: far from it, this is one of the spots where people in the know go to get out of the rat race, usually with a surfboard strapped to the roof of their car.

The beach, black with the fine ironsand typical of this stretch of the west coast of the North Island, is called Sunset Beach for its most striking feature: the glorious blaze of the sunsets that paint the horizon of an evening.

Like Auckland's west coast beaches to the north and Raglan down the coast, Sunset Beach receives the big, muscular Tasman Sea swell, and is at its best in an easterly. It's a long, left-hand bar break, one of the best in the business on its day.

The area was an important source of kai moana for the Maori, and remains a good fishing and shell-fishing spot today. You can try your luck surfcasting for kahawai from the beach, or set-netting for mullet and flounder at the river mouth. The only time the locals will give you a dirty look in these parts is if you produce a whitebaiting frame from the boot of your car between 15 August and 30 November each year: up and down the country, there's a gold rush mentality about these slimy little critters, and everyone has their own possie and set of territorial instincts.

Port Waikato is ideal for a day-trip, but there are accommodation options ranging from the local campground and baches for rent, to farmstays and bed-and-breakfasts. It also works well as a stopover on the road less travelled, down the wild west coast to Raglan.

Port Waikato is a chance to escape from the rat race.

101 MUST-DO'S
FOR KIWIS

Raglan

PHOTO NEW ZEALAND/MIKE HEYDON

Surfers are everywhere but there are plenty of other attractions.

Ask anyone with blonde, salt-draggled hair and the odd piercing where the best surf break in New Zealand is, and there's a fair chance they'll name Raglan without a moment's hesitation. Right in the path of the big, hollow-chested Tasman swell, it enjoys a happy coincidence of landforms and oceanography, 48 kilometres from Hamilton by road and a million miles from anywhere.

The town wasn't actually named after a set of funny sleeves; it was named in the mid-1800s for the commander of the British forces at Crimea (boy, would he have been flattered). In pre-European times, Maori knew this area as a place of healing, and would make their way here to soak in the bracing briny and recharge mind and body.

Since European settlement, it's preserved that reputation, and there's even a health and relaxation spa for women at Whale Bay. Most of those who live here are in full retreat from the bruising pace of modern urban life, and most visitors feel the stress ebbing from their necks and shoulders the minute they come over the hill and around the corner towards Raglan. You don't have to be a surfer to love this place.

You don't *have* to be a surfer, but it helps. Manu Bay, eight kilometres down the road from the township and better known to surfers as The Point, is reputed to deliver one of the most accessible and consistent left-handed breaks in the world. Certainly it offers length of ride — the right wave will keep you up for ten minutes and carry you the best part of two kilometres.

It's a longer paddle out to the line-up at Whale Bay, but once there, you'll find yourself amongst one of the world's great breaks: Indicators, where those big Tasman thumpers peel along a long, long boulder bank.

Don't worry if you're a novice: you can hire a board and get expert tuition at Raglan's renowned surfing academy — grommets are people too, after all — or you can hire boogie board, wetsuit and fins, or just do a spot of body-bashing in the breakers.

There's a heap to do for non-surfers too. There's kayaking, horse riding, even golf, although you'll need to get to grips with an unusual natural hazard in the shape of sheep grazing the fairways. There are cafés, galleries and the local pub. And there's the sunset. Don't forget the sunset — once you've seen it, you won't . . .

I LOVE YOU NEW ZEALAND

Sit on a bench in the Wainui Reserve and take in the view — awesome!
Jason Dawson

Raglan is famous for its left-hand break.

PHOTO NEW ZEALAND

Coromandel & Bay of Plenty

All that glitters is not gold, and while the gold rushes are over, the sparkling waters and dazzling beaches of the Coromandel Peninsula and the Bay of Plenty still draw the crowds. The area's history adds another dimension to a visit and for a real thrill you can poke about on New Zealand's most active volcano. It's the Bay of Plenty all right.

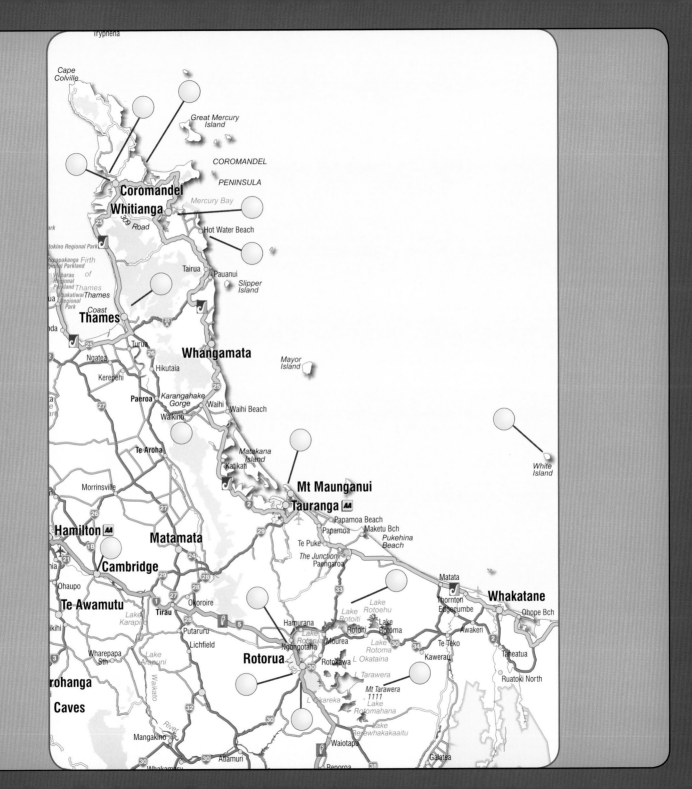

Coromandel Township

Nearly a century after the goldminers, and decades after the bushmen who extracted kauri from the rainforest blanketing the rugged Coromandel Range, the hippies moved in.

It's hard to explain to anyone who hasn't been there exactly what it is that drew whole bouquets of Flower Children to the Coromandel in the 1960s and 1970s. At first glance, it's pretty unpromising country if you're after an easy life off the fat of the land: rugged, stony, heavily forested and on the western side, where Coromandel township is sited, very tidal.

Perhaps it's the stillness of the rainforest, the misty vistas of mountain, headland and sea that called the souls of the commune-founders hither. Perhaps it was the ready availability of cheap land and abundant pot clay. Perhaps it had to do with the camouflage the bush offered their crops, which in those days had more to do with pot than clay.

Whatever the reason, Coromandel — rivalled only by Nelson — was Hippy Central for New Zealand. And while most of the residents of the communes in the 1960s and 1970s spent the 1980s turning on and tuning in to the stockmarket, there are still real hippies living, feral and shy, in and around Coromandel.

The great thing about alternative lifestylers is that they are, to make a sweeping generalisation, creative and unconventional types. Coromandel is

FAVOURITES

BEST SEAFOOD
The Coromandel Smoking Co., 70 Tiki Road, Coromandel

BEST BAIT
The Bait Stop, 2 Kapanga Road, Coromandel

home to a thriving artistic community.

At Driving Creek, for example, just outside the township — named for its role in the kauri extraction days — Barry Brickell has deployed creativity on an industrial scale. He has built a narrow-gauge railway up into the hills from which he mines the clay he uses in his pottery. The railway also takes fare-paying passengers on an unforgettable ride through the rainforest which is studded with ceramic figures from Brickell's studio and offers views over Coromandel Harbour and the Hauraki Gulf beyond.

There are larger and smaller creative enterprises all along this coast. There's also Waiau Waterpark — a well-maintained garden featuring an array of fanciful, water-powered gadgets that you're encouraged to fool about with.

Up in the hills, on your way over to the east coast if you're taking the main road, or a short detour if you're going all the way to Cape Colville, there's Castle Rock Winery in the Te Rerenga Valley, which specialises in fruit and vegetable wines. How hippy is that?

Coromandel township still has an air of the gold-rush days.

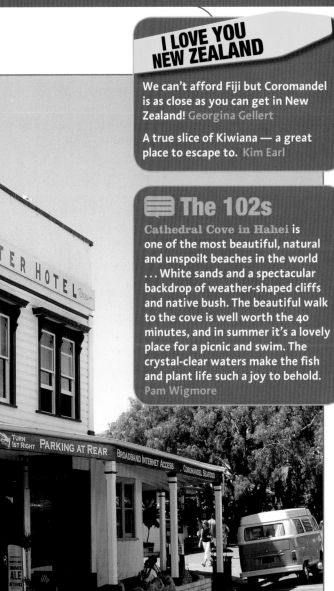

PHOTO NEW ZEALAND/MIKE CLARE

I LOVE YOU NEW ZEALAND

We can't afford Fiji but Coromandel is as close as you can get in New Zealand! Georgina Gellert

A true slice of Kiwiana — a great place to escape to. Kim Earl

The 102s

Cathedral Cove in Hahei is one of the most beautiful, natural and unspoilt beaches in the world … White sands and a spectacular backdrop of weather-shaped cliffs and native bush. The beautiful walk to the cove is well worth the 40 minutes, and in summer it's a lovely place for a picnic and swim. The crystal-clear waters make the fish and plant life such a joy to behold. Pam Wigmore

Hot Water Beach

The entire eastern coastline of the Coromandel Peninsula is studded with jewel-like beaches. The sand is white, the pohutukawa crimson, the water warm and clear . . . What, you ask, could be nicer?

Drop in to Hot Water Beach, about 35 kilometres down the coast from Whitianga, and you'll find out. But remember to take a spade: a bucket is optional, but a garden spade or contractor's shovel is not.

The name probably gives the game away, but the distinguishing feature of Hot Water Beach is the hot water that you can uncover by shifting a few inches of sand in the intertidal zone.

The Coromandel Range marks the line of a volcanic fault. Geologically speaking it is continuous with the Kaimais, the range that separates the Waikato from the Bay of Plenty and the fault terminates, significantly as it seems, in the geothermal wonderland of Rotorua. There's some fringe benefits to living smack bang on top of the volcanic Ring of Fire, and New Zealand's geothermal resources is one of these.

There are several hot springs in this area, dotted along the line of the fault. Sapphire Springs, just north of Katikati, is one example. The springs at Te Aroha and at Miranda on the Firth of Thames are others. Hot Water Beach draws its heated water, broadly speaking, from the same source.

Come here a couple of hours either side of low water and you'll see any number of people — individuals and groups — digging for all they're worth. As the holes deepen, they fill with water, and once everyone reckons they've dug down far enough for a decent soak, it's time to down tools and pile in.

Everyone lies there happily for a while. Then it's not uncommon to see a new round of earthworks commence as overheated soakers drive trenches to the low-tide mark, to induce cooler water into their tubs to lower the temperature a bit.

The view from your improvised hot tub is pretty gratifying too. You can contemplate the wide Pacific horizon out there beyond Castle Island, and the nice, clean swell that Hot Water Beach gets on its day. And of course, if you have too much of a good thing, you can always make a dash for the surf to cool off, although make sure you swim between the flags as this beach can be dangerous.

Eventually, the incoming tide overwhelms the thermal zone, and the waves erase all traces of the enthusiasm of that session's balneologists.

A beach with hot and cold running water: how cool — or hot — is that?

PHOTO NEW ZEALAND/NICK SERVIAN

📑 The 102s

For a break away you can't go past
Te Aroha. Mount Te Aroha is a
beacon in the Kaimai Ranges. Do as
much or as little as you want. Climb
the mountain and you feel like
you're standing on top of the world
and if you catch a sunset from the
summit . . . magic! There's mountain
biking, the Heritage Domain, and
lovely hot soda spas. Michele Laurie

A frenzy of
diggers sets in
at Hot Water
Beach as the tide
recedes.

101 MUST-DO'S
FOR KIWIS

Karangahake Gorge

If a day weeding the garden leaves you laid up with backache for a week, spare a thought for the hard folk who left their mark on the landscape wherever a sniff of gold was detected.

The rock of the Coromandel Peninsula is honeycombed with shafts and tunnels driven and sunk by men with equipment no more sophisticated than you'd deploy in your vege patch — pick, shovel and wheelbarrow — although unlike most recreational gardeners, some did have occasional recourse to dynamite.

Some of the best preserved workings of the Coromandel district gold rush of the late 1860s — the last significant occasion on which the discovery of gold led men to descend en masse to a New Zealand locality — can be seen in the pretty Karangahake Gorge, between Paeroa and Waihi at the base of the Coromandel Peninsula.

The trouble with the gold in these here hills was that unlike the alluvial stuff of the South Island, this was all lode-borne, found in veins shot through quartz, that in turn formed seams in the Coromandel's iron-hard granite. Extracting it was no simple matter of scooping up a few shovelfuls of sand and gravel and swirling it about in your pan. Oh no: first you had to accomplish with your gardening tools what the awesome forces of nature had taken aeons to do in alluvial fields — break the rock, extract the quartz and crush it to get at the gold.

The gold-bearing quartz in the hills through which the Ohinemuri River cuts its way was liberated by blasting and chipping it out bodily using pick and shovel. It was then conveyed to stamper batteries which, as their name suggests, were great steam-powered hammers designed to pulverise rock to dust. The remains of three of these can be seen in the Karangahake Gorge. Access to them is by an easy, well-graded four and a half kilometre walkway, which follows the same route as the railway that once ran from Paeroa to the Waihi goldmine. This includes a couple of historic bridges and a one kilometre tunnel, sporting side shafts blasted through the tunnel walls to the exterior, namely the cliffs fronting the Waitewheta River. These shafts were originally built to allow waste rock to be cast out of the mine, but now they serve as picture windows for sightseers.

In summer, you can round off the half-day's exploration of the railway and the gold workings with a picnic lunch and a swim in one of the Ohinemuri's lazy pools. Now that's a solid gold experience.

PHOTO NEW ZEALAND

Owharoa Falls,
Karangahake
Gorge.

101 MUST-DO'S
FOR KIWIS

Mount Maunganui: Mauao

BAY OF PLENTY TOURISM

Mount Maunganui marks the entrance to the Tauranga Harbour and the start of a string of white beaches.

FAVOURITES

BEST ICE CREAM
Skoops Ice Cream Bar, Domain Road

BEST CAMPSITE
Mount Maunganui Domain Motor Camp

BEST ESCAPE IN WINTER
Mount Maunganui Hot Salt Water Pools, Adams Avenue

BEST COFFEE
Slowfish, Marine Parade

The proper Maori name of Mount Maunganui — or 'the Mount', as most New Zealanders tend to call it these days — has a certain poetry that Maunganui ('big hill') does not. Mauao means 'caught in the light of the day', alluding to the Arawa story of how the hill came to be where it is, isolated at the end of the peninsula that forms the southern headland of the entrance to Tauranga Harbour.

The legend is a version of that eternal story: the love triangle. Poor old Mauao was once pononga (a slave) to a mountain called Otanewainuku, situated about 40 kilometres due south of Tauranga, the highest point in the Mamaku Range. The slave hill, then nameless, was in love with Puwhena, but she was already

BAY OF PLENTY TOURISM

The walk at the base of the Mount is popular year round.

Otanewainuku's special hill-friend and therefore spoken for.

What's a heartbroken, love-lorn hill to do? He resolved to drown himself in the Pacific, and enlisted the patupaiarehe, fairies, to help him do it. He cast a spell to make himself portable for a limited time, and the fairy folk obligingly set about dragging him toward the ocean. Typical tradesmen, they didn't quite get the job done in time, and when they vanished back to the depot (or wherever nocturnal fairies hang out in daytime), dawn found the jilted lover yards from his watery objective. With the first touch of sunlight, the spell wore off and Tauranga acquired the cocked silhouette of its most striking landmark, while the Kaimais were left with a space where the sad old hill used to be.

Of course, geologists will tell you that Mauao is really the remnants of a rhyolite volcanic cone, but where's the romance in that?

Generations of Kiwis have come in the summer to enjoy the superb surf beach, the three and a half kilometre track around the foot of Mount Maunganui and the peerless view of the Bay of Plenty and Tauranga Harbour from the Mount's 231 metre summit.

Prosperity arrived here in the 1950s, in the shape of the happy coincidence of an Asian building boom, the maturity of millions of hectares of pine forest on the Central Plateau and the decision to locate New Zealand's fourth export port on the Mount Maunganui peninsula. Since then, the fibrolite baches that once fronted the beach have been overshadowed by palatial holiday homes and high-rise apartment buildings. Many people now live there year round, but it's still a summer town at heart.

Mauao the volcano may be extinct, but come here at New Year's Eve and witness a whole new meaning to the term 'going off'.

New Chums Beach

The east coast of the Coromandel Peninsula has more than its fair share of pretty beaches. For generations, Kiwis built their baches there — little one-room, fibrolite or board-and-batten buildings with long-drop toilet out back — within spitting distance of the dunes and the gorgeous beach beyond.

The latest generation of bach-builders have gone about it slightly differently. If fibrolite or board-and-batten is used, it tends these days to be an architect's sardonic pun on the concept of the Kiwi bach. Most of the 'holiday homes' flung up lately in Pauanui or Matarangi, for example, tend to have more king-sized bedrooms with en-suites than the traditional bach had bunks. Stucco is the cladding of choice, and the sunset over the lovely, switchback skyline of the Coromandel Range is reflected in smoked-glass windows and stainless steel balustrades. Swimming pools are now de rigueur, for those days when 100 metres is too far to walk, or the sea is just too salty, or something.

That has been the fate of the majority of the Coromandel beaches. Happily, though, there are still one or two that have escaped the developer's eye. Cathedral Cove is one example. New Chums Beach is another.

In fact, British newspaper, *The Observer*, recently ranked the latter as one of the 20 best deserted beaches in the world. New Chums Beach is in Wainuiototo Bay, handy to both Whitianga and Coromandel townships. To get there, you'll need to drive to Whangapoua Beach and then hoof it. It's about a 30-minute walk, which begins with a wade through the estuary at the northern end of Whangapoua Beach at low tide. A track crosses a saddle over the southern headland, and there you are, overlooking a classically-formed stretch of dazzling white sand, backed with pohutukawa-fringed bush.

Shellfish can be gathered here (and in the Whangapoua estuary on the way). What a spot for a picnic, a swim and a bit of basking in the sun. But get in quick. There are already plans afoot to subdivide the land behind New Chums Beach, and yet another slice of paradise will be lost to us. It's now or never!

CLAIRE SMITH

New Chums Beach has thankfully, so far, escaped the developer's eye.

The Pinnacles

It's hard to argue that the coming of Europeans was a good thing for the Coromandel Peninsula. As soon as the first tall-masted ships appeared, the fate of the mature kauri forest blanketing the peninsula was as good as sealed. Logging got going in a big way, the timber mustered behind dams across the beds of the steep creeks descending from the peninsula's high spine to the coast, and then released in 'drives' that carried the massive tree trunks booming and crashing down on the flood.

You can see remnants of this activity — and of the goldminers' workings — on the Kauaeranga Valley loop track, a relatively easy three-day walk with one night in a hut and the other in your tent at one of the designated Department of Conservation campgrounds. Er . . . you did pack your tent, didn't you?

The first section of the track, assuming you tackle the Moss Creek route first, takes you over a classic New Zealand backcountry suspension bridge, through nikau and rata groves — the latter a spectacular sight when the crimson rata is in blossom — and then climbs steadily to the spot where Moss Creek Hut stood until it burned down in 1993. Here, you'll camp for your first night. If you still have the energy on the approach to the campsite, or if you want a bit of a warm up in the morning, consider making the side trip to Mount Rowe, which rewards those who tackle the muddy scramble to its summit with superb views of the Firth of Thames and the rugged Coromandel Range. Near the campsite itself, there are remnants of two kauri dams, which are also worth a visit.

On the second day, the track joins what used to be a packhorse route across the ranges to Coroglen (known as Gumtown in the gumdigging days), and flirts with the Kauaeranga River on its way up to the superb new hut in the shadow of the Pinnacles. The best of the kauri dams in the Valley, the Dancing Creek dam, is close to the Pinnacles Hut. The Pinnacles themselves are a further 50 minutes of clambering, slipping and slithering in the bad bits, and scrambling up the ladders that have been laid over the worst. The views from the top of the rugged Pinnacles make it all worthwhile.

Keep an eye on the weather in this part of the country: there are numerous stream and river crossings, and these have a habit of swelling rapidly in rain.

The 102s

Visit Coroglen and go horseback riding at Rangihau Ranch. I found the tracks great and the views absolutely breathtaking — one of the tracks is an old mail route. You get to see for miles and experience real New Zealand bush and countryside. And after your ride you can cruise on down to the Coroglen Pub for a cool drink and something to eat.

Sandy Rawlings

Trampers crossing a stream in the Kauaeranga Valley.

101 MUST-DO'S FOR KIWIS

White Island

Volcanoes are a bit like big dogs. However well you might think you know them, however dopey and friendly they might seem, there's always the chance they'll go bad, and if they do, look out.

Some volcanoes, of course, are stroppier than others. A stroll on Mount Eden, for example, feels safe. A poke around on the flanks of Whakaari — White Island — by contrast, does not.

That's because White Island is the most obviously active of our volcanoes. Mount Ruapehu and Mount Ngauruhoe have a history of waking suddenly and with very little warning, catching everyone by surprise. On the other hand, if you were to be so unfortunate as to be in the way when White Island blew its top, it'd be hard to argue you weren't warned. In big dog terms, White Island has a permanent snarl twisting its lips, and slobber hanging from its jaws.

Of course, that's what makes it so much fun to visit. It takes around 80 minutes to get there by boat — far less by helicopter — landing in Crater Bay. On the way, you'll be issued with a gas mask and a hard hat, which will make you feel really safe.

Once ashore, you're greeted by a moonscape of volcanic desolation, with the melancholy, rusted remains of a sulphur factory visible at the terminus of the mudflow that overwhelmed it, taking 11 lives, in 1914.

One of the unique features of White Island is that there is no exhausting

I LOVE YOU NEW ZEALAND

So it's a volcano, and you get to walk around it! In a bizarre-looking gas face mask thing. Brilliant! Scary, thrilling, beautiful, edgy, fun, educational, interesting, and an ideal set for the next James Bond movie. *Kylie Cotter*

climb up sliding scree slopes or flinty lava flows to get to where the action is. Access to the central crater is a short stroll over packed dirt that may as well be flat. It takes you past hot springs and mini geysers, and fissures in the rock through which steam hisses. Active fumaroles de-gas in the middle of the crater area itself, earning themselves names such as Donald Duck and Noisy Nellie, and the sulphuric stink of geothermal activity hangs over everything.

A crater lake is intermittently present over the site of recent activity: this changes colour depending on the weather and the mood of the volcano, from milky grey to vivid green or azure blue.

It's a harsh environment for precious belongings such as digital cameras: you might like to take a disposable instead. One thing is certain: you'll want to take photographs. A walk on White Island is a once-in-a-lifetime experience.

PHOTO NEW ZEALAND/CHRIS CAMERON

Volcanic White
Island looks
relatively benign
from the air.

Rotorua & Waitomo

There's more to Rotorua than hot springs, boiling mud pools, geysers and volcanic remains, although these are fascinating enough. Visitors can get a unique window on the Maori world at Whakarewarewa. You can get a rush over the highest commercially rafted falls in the world, or a thrill on Rotorua's Luge and Sky Swing. Similarly, there's more to Waitomo than the big wet hole for which it's named. Read on . . .

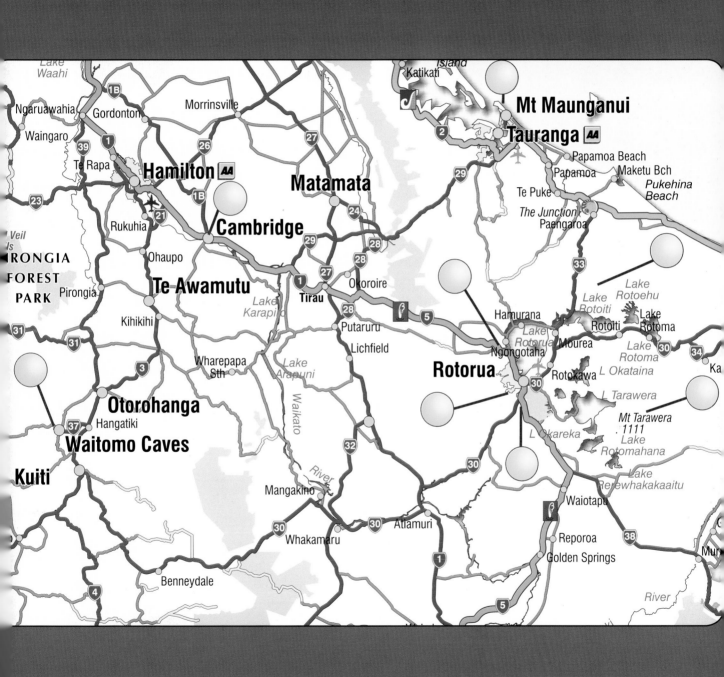

Mount Tarawera

Lake Tarawera, at the foot of the mountain of the same name, is the site of one of New Zealand's creepiest ghost stories. On the morning of 31 May 1886, just as the mist was rising from the lake, a pair of sightseeing parties set out across the water. Their Maori guides were reluctant, because the lake was acting strangely: as the boats were preparing to take on their passengers, the water level rose suddenly by more than a metre then sank just as rapidly. It took some fast talking and, one suspects, the greasing of palms before the European passengers were able to persuade their boatmen to proceed.

While they were out on the water, both groups saw a large waka taua being paddled toward the mountain. The occupants wore full ceremonial dress and the greenery of mourning. Their crew called out to the paddlers, but there was no reply. As they watched, waka and crew disappeared into the mist.

All agreed it was a magnificent sight, but the local Maori later pointed out that no such vessel had ever graced the lake, or at least not within living memory. They were perfectly certain that this was an omen of the direst possible kind.

Anyone who scoffed would have felt a mite silly when 11 days later, on the night of 10 June, Mount Tarawera launched into a violent six-hour eruption that tore the mountain apart, drained a lake, buried the famous Pink and White Terraces along with three villages and killed an estimated 153 people. It was the worst natural disaster in New Zealand's recorded history.

Both stories — the phantom canoe and the deadly eruption — add a frisson to any visit to the dark waters of Lake Tarawera, or the blasted remnants of the mountain itself. The area draws thousands of visitors. The summit ridge of the volcano is a wearying scramble up fans of scree, the reward being spectacular views and the exhilarating return journey down the rolling, rattling cinder slope. If you can stand a few bumps and grazes, then the way to tackle it is by mountain bike.

There are several picnic spots dotted around the shores of the lake. One of these, at Hot Water Beach, is adjacent to an area of submerged springs and fumaroles, and if you pick your spot, you can have a hot bath over sand heated by the same thermal engine that drove the Tarawera eruption. Choose wisely, though: anglers who get lucky with the local trout use areas of the thermally heated sand to cook their catch. Mind where you put your feet.

PHOTO NEW ZEALAND

I LOVE YOU NEW ZEALAND

I have climbed this mountain five times and it is awesome: hard going up, easy coming down. When you get to the top there is a fine gravel dip leading to the crater. If you can find this, step back about 15 metres and run and leap into the air when you get to the edge . . . you'll sink into the gravel up to your waist.
Sheree Clarke

Scoria and rocks at the top of the crater of Mount Tarawera.

65

Rotorua Geothermal Wonders

Back in the day, no one thought very much of Rotorua. The real action was nearby at the little township of Ohinemutu, from which you could hire a waka and a guide to take you to the Pink and White Terraces. Rotorua was known as the 'Rotten Egg Town'.

When the Duke of Edinburgh visited in 1870 to 'take the waters', however, the government realised just how deeply people believed in the healing powers of thermal springs and hot mud. Rotorua — which had hot water and boiling bogs to burn — suddenly began to look like a tourist bonanza waiting to happen. The government appointed an official balneologist, and set about developing Rotten Egg Town as a health spa.

Although the Bathhouse that was the focal point of that original health spa now serves as a museum, there are still spa facilities in and around Rotorua. One of the most popular is located in the Hell's Gate geothermal reserve.

Before you take the plunge, you can have a poke around the park. Like many parts of the landscape around Rotorua, fumaroles and mini-geysers pock the ground everywhere — after all, this is a town where even the stormwater drains in the street pour forth steam. There's a lively mud pool called the Devil's Cauldron, which cheerfully belches. There's a mini-volcano that spurts globules of mud into the air. There's a thermally fed waterfall,

the highest in the southern hemisphere, and alongside this, there's the spa, where you can immerse yourself in hot, mineral-rich mud, soak in sulphurous pools, and afterwards enjoy an invigorating session of mirimiri, or traditional massage.

Also in the wider Rotorua area, there's the fascinating Waimangu Volcanic Valley, where you can see the Frying Pan Lake, the largest hot spring in the world, at a high simmer. There's also what looks for all the world like a large swimming pool, turquoise blue, 30 metres across and surrounded by fluted limestone walls. The name gives the game away. If anyone asked you whether you fancied a dip in the Inferno Crater, what do you suppose your answer would be? Safer to stick to Hell's Gate, just as the therapeutic mud of Hell's Gate sticks to you.

Take the time to check out the Champagne Pool at Wai-o-tapu, 20 minutes south of Rotorua.

PHAEDRA CADNESS

Also experience the full force of the Wai-o-tapu geyser.

67

101 MUST-DO'S FOR KIWIS

Rotorua Luge, Skyrides & Sky Swing

In the Winter Olympics luge event, the athlete reclines on a light toboggan that he or she pilots down the hillside in a twisting, snaking ice gutter. There wasn't much prospect of creating an ice gutter on Mount Ngongotaha, just outside Rotorua, as it only snows there maybe once every winter. But why, some can-do Kiwi reasoned, should that stop us. We can overcome the lack of a suitable climate as Kiwis have surmounted all manner of problems down through the ages — with concrete.

You ride the Rotorua luge on three-wheeled plastic trolleys, which have a clever gravity-operated braking system and remarkably responsive steering.

The original track was a screamer. It began gently enough, but through a tunnel, round a corner and you suddenly encountered a change in gradient that would have the unwary — or the intrepid — airborne.

Down the steep pitch you went and at the bottom you were confronted with a choice: the great, sweeping, sharply cambered 'fast lane', or the rather more sedate 'slow lane'.

Everyone took the fast lane, of course. It was a matter of holding your nerve, letting the laws of physics hold you into the turn. Trouble was, right after you exited the elbow of the fast lane, you were confronted with a tight left-hander and a convergence with the slow lane. It wasn't pretty at this point, especially in those early days before the national mania for occupational health and safety issues set in. No safety gear, not even bicycle helmets, was issued back then.

Now, though, the operators have cottoned on to the simple business logic that says customers who survive the experience without being seriously injured are not only more capable of coming back for more but also more inclined to.

These days, there are three tracks you can choose: the 'Advanced' which is a kilometre long; the one and a half kilometre 'Intermediate', where you can take things a bit more quietly; and the 'Scenic', which winds its sedate way down through the mighty redwoods, offering spectacular views of the wider Rotorua district on the way, and is even suitable for small children. The Intermediate and Scenic routes are lit for night-time descents. Between rides you get to enjoy the views from the chairlift which gives access to the top of Mount Ngongotaha.

Five million people have ridden the luge since it opened, and it's a rush to remember. They'll swear by it . . .

SKYLINE SKYRIDES

Head to the top of Mount Ngongotaha in style and get your thrills on the luge on the way back down.

69

101 MUST-DO'S FOR KIWIS

Rotorua Rafting

The upper reaches of the Kaituna River are pretty and placid enough. In between bursts of frenetic paddling and brief flurries of white water, you'll probably have time to admire the country through which the river meanders, putting the 'gorge' in 'gorgeous' all the way.

The bush overhangs the water, and the banks are pocked with caves. The entire area is significant to the Arawa, the local iwi, and every bend in the river and hole in the rock has its place in myth and legend. The guides relate some of the stories to you, and indicate points of interest as you pass.

While they seemed pleasant enough on dry land and on the drive out to the drop-in point, you swiftly discover that rafting guides are actually the direct descendants of the types the Romans used to employ to keep their galley-slaves earning their gruel. Fortunately, in these enlightened days, occupational safety and health considerations prevent them using a cat-o'-nine-tails to keep the tempo up, but there's little short of the lash that they won't resort to in their quest for paddle speed when the water whitens up.

Here and there, the guides refresh your memory on some of the finer points of the safety briefing they delivered at the beginning of the trip. You've been through a few rapids by now, you've felt the muscles of the river through the canvas floor of the boat, nothing you couldn't handle. So what's all the fuss about?

I LOVE YOU NEW ZEALAND

The most fun I ever had in a wet suit.
Marie O'Brien

If you've been paying attention, you'll have noticed, scattered through their patter, the odd mention of something they refer to only as 'the Big One'. Some monster of the Kaituna, you're led to believe, something waiting downstream from here. Something to be reckoned with.

And once you're gasping, shaken and stirred, at the foot of the first waterfall, and the guides have explained it's a tiddler compared to 'the Big One', then you start to get a sense of what you might be in for. And soon enough, it's upon you.

There's a bit of frantic paddling to do to get the boat all lined up, then at your guide's invitation, you ship your paddle, get down in the bottom of the boat and hold tight to the safety rope. And over you go, over 'the Big One', the highest commercially rafted waterfall in the southern hemisphere and the reason the Kaituna is grade-five water (grade one is flat; grade five is not). Wet, wild — and wonderful.

PHOTO NEW ZEALAND

Rafting the 'Big One', the seven metre Tutea Falls on the Kaituna River.

101 MUST-DO'S FOR KIWIS

Waitomo Caves

It's not everyone's idea of fun, grovelling about in cold mud in holes in the rock with mere inches of wriggle room on either side, the only illumination cast by your headlamp.

Inevitably, though, there's a section of our society for whom this is their very definition of a cracking good time, and the place to go get it in the North Island is Waitomo, about 50 kilometres south-west of Hamilton.

Waitomo's name, loosely translated, is 'wet hole'. But you don't have to be half-man/half-worm to enjoy the wonders of Waitomo. There's a range of activities — from the sedate to borderline suicidal — to suit all ages, agilities, temperaments and tolerances for enclosed spaces.

Set in a weird and wonderful tract of karst landscape — where weathered limestone and marble outcrops form outlandish shapes on the surface — the caves have been a tourist drawcard since the early days of European settlement.

Perhaps the best known and most popular of Waitomo's charms is the Glow-worm Caves, a massive cavern system on three levels, bejewelled with minerals and hung the whole ceiling over with the cold, blue fairy-lights of glow-worms. These

Try the Haggas Honking Holes at Waitomo Adventures . . .

WWW.WAITOMO.CO.NZ

are the larvae of *Arachnocampa luminosa*, a fungus-munching bug, that use the light they emit to attract the other tiny insects upon which they prey.

The first level of the Glow-worm Cave features a cave called the Banquet Chamber, as it was the luncheon-stop for early visitors to the caves: you can still see traces of tobacco smoke staining the ceiling. This level also features a cavern graced with great fluted stalactites and stalagmites, which is aptly named the Pipe Organ.

Down on the second level of the caves is the largest cavern, which is called The Cathedral as a nod to its high, vaulted ceiling and angelic acoustics.

There are countless other caves in the Waitomo area. Aranui Cave was named for the young Maori man who found it while in hot pursuit of a pig. It features structures with the evocative names of Fairy Walk, Temple of Peace, Aladdin's Cave and Eastern Scene.

And then there's Mangapu, a 100 metre tomo (vertical shaft) into which visitors with no previous experience can abseil. The sunlight reaches the floor of this deep hole, and picks out threads of mist hanging in the twilight and tendrils of plants clinging to the walls. The *Lonely Planet* guidebook has called the 'Lost World' tour of Mangapu 'one of the most amazing things you can do in the country'. To find out why, you'll have to try it for yourself.

And if that isn't wet or racy enough for you, there's always black-water rafting through the Ruakuri Cavern.

Buried alive — and loving it.

... or St Benedicts Cavern ...

... and enjoy the wonders of Waitomo.

Whakarewarewa

When you consider how hard it must have been to make the transition from their tropical homeland to the decidedly sub-tropical rigours of the New Zealand climate, you can immediately understand why the first Polynesian settlers were attracted to the Whakarewarewa valley. There was hot and cold — mostly hot — running water, spa baths, inbuilt cooking facilities and the entire valley featured underfloor heating. Luxury.

When the region overdid the whole geothermal thing in 1886 and Mount Tarawera destroyed the Pink and White Terraces, the raison d'être of their thriving niche in the tourism industry, the Tuhourangi and Ngati Wahiao sub-tribes of Arawa upped sticks and shifted to Whakarewarewa, to try again with the natural attractions of the valley. It was a bit of a hit.

With fumaroles hissing, mud pools snorting and one of the seven geysers in the area letting fly every so often, visitors just couldn't get enough. The displaced hapu made Whaka their home — and they're still there.

Today, Whakarewarewa is a sophisticated tourist operation, featuring not only the thermal area — with the famous Pohutu and Prince of Wales geysers — but also the well-designed cultural centre, Te Puia.

Named for the undefeated fortress of the Arawa people, Te Puia provides an interface between visitors and Maori culture. It includes the New Zealand Institute of Maori Arts and Crafts, where traditional woodcarving and flax-weaving are practised. There are cultural performances twice daily, showcasing Maori song, dance and story. They'll even provide you with dinner, cooked in a hangi where no fire was necessary.

Korero Tuku Iho tours are designed to introduce visitors to Te Ao Maori, and to the world of Te Arawa in particular, by guiding them through the natural wonders of the geothermal area, the bush and the kiwi house, while the guides relate the legends and lore of the people of the land.

Best of all, just as they don't turn off the geysers and throw covers over the mud pools of an evening, nor do all the guides at Whaka clock out at the great gate, or waharoa, jump in their cars and drive home at the end of the working day. Many of them live here. Whakarewarewa is their home, and they're proud to show it off.

PHOTO NEW ZEALAND

The residents at
Whakarewarewa
are proud to
showcase their
culture.

101 MUST-DO'S
FOR KIWIS

6 Eastland

From the rugged heartland of the North Island's Eastland to the glorious beaches of fringing Poverty Bay and the East Cape, there's something in this region to please everyone. Tramping in the Urewera National Park, slithering down the Rere rock slide, sipping a Gisborne chardonnay, touring East Cape or just lying on the beach . . . Poverty Bay? Yeah, right.

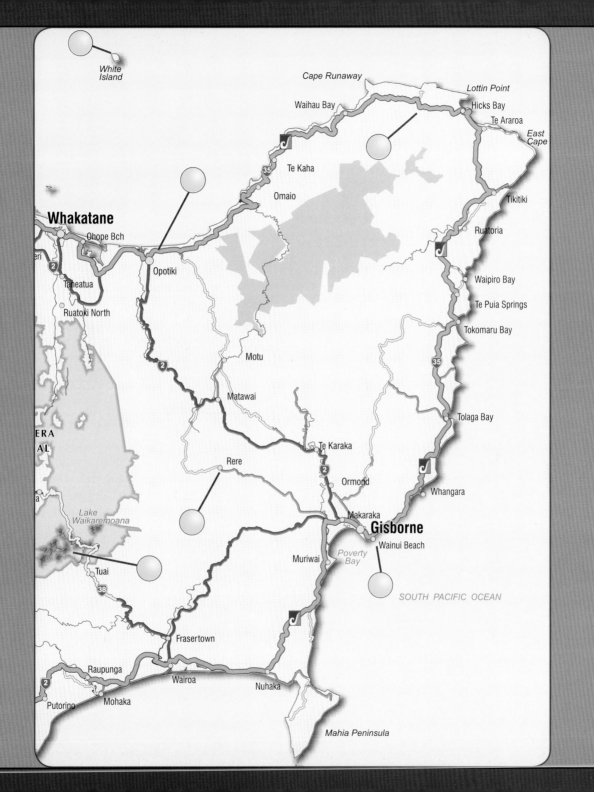

Eastland

There's a lot to be said for sticking to State Highway 2 when travelling around the eastern part of the North Island, and most of it involves the scenic splendours of the Waioeka Gorge.

If you've got a bit of time to spare, however, and preferably more than the six hours it takes to do it in one looking-neither-left-nor-right hit, then you'd be mad if you didn't take the long way round the coast, State Highway 35.

You face the decision in Gisborne, and once you've made the right choice, you'll find yourself cruising back in time to the days before great swathes of the North Island coast began to resemble a kind of seaside Pakuranga. And here's the good news: there's over 300 kilometres of underpopulated coastline ahead, with plenty to do along the way.

The stretch of rocky coast just up the road from Gisborne is one of the few areas in New Zealand which still welcomes freedom camping — where you can park your motor home or pitch a tent by the side of the road for free.

One of the wide, white-sand beaches you'll come to on the haul north is Tolaga Bay, where the long, long —the longest, in fact, in New Zealand — concrete wharf projects far out into the rollers. This is a solid reminder of the days when most of New Zealand's transport needs were met by coastal shipping, and passengers, farm supplies and produce alike made

The 102s

Try **Port Awanui**, 12 kilometres seaward from Ruatoria: awesome beach, great fishing and no people.
Lesley Fisher

their inward and outward journeys by steamer and via wharves such as these.

Just north of Tolaga Bay, there's another such reminder at Tokomaru Bay, where the crumbling remains of shipping company buildings, offices, warehouses and bond stores are testimony to just how important the coastal trade was.

After a soak in the thermal waters of Te Puia Springs, you can stop for refreshments at Ruatoria, then press on to Te Araroa, New Zealand's easternmost settlement. If you're up for a bit of a detour, the East Cape lighthouse is just a 40 kilometre round trip, not counting the 700-odd steps you climb to reach the lonely lighthouse itself.

The beaches along the western flank of the cape are dazzling, as is the fishing, if you're of a mind to stop and try your luck. And if you want to wash the salt off before you reach the bright lights of Opotoki and the Bay of Plenty beyond, you can have a dip in the swift waters of the Motu River.

PHOTO NEW ZEALAND/IAN TRAFFORD

Check out
New Zealand's
longest concrete
wharf at
Tolaga Bay.

101 MUST-DO'S
FOR KIWIS

Lake Waikaremoana

Urewera, according to eye-watering local legend, was named to commemorate a nocturnal incident involving the leader of a war party, someone else's wife and the painful conjunction of his nether regions with a campfire.

The rugged, forested expanse is also New Zealand's third largest national park, boasting the largest untouched swathe of bush in the North Island, which is the legacy of the often touchy relationship through time between the local iwi, Tuhoe, 'the people of the mist', and the Crown. Deer and pigs abound here, and the dense, luxuriant rainforest forms a handsome setting for the gem that is Waikaremoana, 'the lake of rippling waters'.

The track that performs a half-circuit around the lake is one of New Zealand's ten Great Walks, and makes for an unforgettable tramping experience. It covers a total distance of 46 kilometres, and while there are seven huts en route, it can be covered in a relatively easy four days.

The track can be tackled from either direction, but if anyone tries to tell you to do it from the Onepoto Bay end, disregard their advice and shun them as fools thereafter. Far better to start at Hopuruahine Landing, so that by the time you tackle the formidable climb to Panekiri Bluff on the second-to-last day, your pack is much lighter.

Waikaremoana was formed when a landslide triggered by an earthquake dammed the tributaries of the Waikare-Taheke River. Divers and grumpy anglers report a sunken petrified forest at one end of the lake. The walk follows the foreshore on flat or undulating terrain, until that final gasping ascent through

the tortured and moss-bedecked forms of ancient beech trees to Panekiri Bluff, which commands a gob smacking view over the lake and the deep green Urewera ranges. At Onepoto Bay, the outlet to the track, there are the remains of an armed constabulary redoubt and the tombstones of soldiers who were killed there in one episode of the aforementioned touchy relationship between Tuhoe and the Crown.

The lake has great fishing, and if you don't feel up to walking the entire track you can get a water-taxi to pick you up or drop you off on sections of it, such as at the entrance to the short but rewarding walk up to Lake Waikareiti.

The wider Te Urewera National Park offers plenty of other short or long walks, and the hunting is as superb as the terrain is challenging. And never mind all that physical stuff, one of the great beauties of the Urewera is just how pretty the roads are, in and out.

The Urewera — enjoy, but mind that campfire.

Lake Waikaremoana and Panekire Bluff from Lou's Lookout.

PHOTO NEW ZEALAND/IAN TRAFFORD

Rere Rock Slide

We'll let you in on a little secret here, so long as you promise not to let it go any further. It's a secret jealously guarded by the close-knit, boogie-boarding fraternity of Eastland. When they're done frolicking in the surf at Wainui Beach (or on the rare days when Wainui is serving nothing but mush), they will load their boards and a picnic lunch in the boots of their HQ Holdens and head for the hills, travelling west on the Wharekopae Road, checking their mirrors every now and then to make sure they're not being followed.

Their destination lies 50 kilometres along this road, under the shadow of Ngatapa, the site of a hill fortress constructed by the warrior chief, Te Kooti Rikirangi te Turuki, during his insurgency in the 1860s.

It's a little reserve that incorporates the Rere Falls on the Wharekopae River, with a grassy picnic area complete with toilets alongside the river.

The Rere Falls are pretty, but you don't see the boarders wasting too much time looking them over. They're more interested in something upstream. For a little way up the stony riverbed, you'll find the Rere rock slide, a 60 metre tract of slick rock, made slippery by the swift, shallow water flowing over it.

Throw yourself onto your belly on your boogie-board at the top of the slide and hang on for an exhilarating, wet and wild ride to the bottom. It's not steep, but what it lacks in gradient it also lacks in friction. You'll be flying — just make sure you stop short of the falls.

If you don't have a boogie-board, you'd do well to take an inflatable mattress or inner tube or similar, but even then there's a limit to how many times you can bash your body down the slide in a single session. Subtle undulations in the rock deliver a stringent massage, and you'll be feeling it after a few runs. But you don't have to be an extreme sports fanatic to shoot the slide and love it.

If, however, it seems just too gnarly for all in your party, you can pack the frail and faint of heart off to the Eastwood Arboretum, an extraordinary privately established botanical museum that features the largest collection of exotic trees in New Zealand.

When everyone meets up afterwards to compare notes, it'll be hard to decide who had the better time.

Hang on to your shorts on the Rere Rock Slide.

101 MUST-DO'S
FOR KIWIS

Wainui Beach

Because he came from the west, Cook encountered the eastern side of New Zealand's North Island first. The white headland at the southern end of what Cook misnamed Poverty Bay was spied from the *Endeavour's* rigging by cabin boy Nicholas Young — and Young Nick's Head bears his name to this day.

Daylight approaches from the same direction, and thanks to New Zealand's proximity to the International Dateline,

the first city in the world to see the sunrise on each new day is our very own Gisborne. That's what made it a mecca for merrymakers when the new millennium ticked over. Those who stood on Wainui Beach just to the city's north and sipped local chardonnay as the sun heaved over the horizon that morning felt themselves to be among the luckiest people in the world.

Wainui is a beautiful stretch of white sand that receives a nice, clean Pacific swell

Wainui Beach is a surfer's mecca.

PHOTO NEW ZEALAND/IAN TRAFFORD

PHOTO NEW ZEALAND/IAN TRAFFORD

The Gisborne region is the first to see the sun each day.

in westerly weather — and happily, the prevailing winds are from the westerly quarter. And with nothing between spectators and South America but the wide, wide horizon, the sunrises are without peer.

Inland from Gisborne, the alluvial plains are among the most fertile wine-growing soils in New Zealand. Wine was first grown there when a band of Marist missionaries landed in Gisborne instead of their intended destination, Hawke's Bay, in 1850. They planted a few vines before they realised their mistake. A hundred years later, there were a couple of growers scratching their heads at the massive yields from their white grape vines. And 50 years later again, Gisborne has become New Zealand's third largest wine-growing region. White grapes predominate, with chardonnay making up over half of the region's vines. But other varietals are doing well, too — notably gewürtztraminer — and others, such as muscat, viognier, and merlot, show promise.

The best time to appreciate this aspect of our most easterly city is during Gisborne's Wine Week, when events such as the International Chardonnay Challenge — featuring the hard-to-resist Italian Long Lunch — and the Gisborne Wine and Food Festival are celebrated. But wine tours are available at any time of year, and Gisborne's climate is highly conducive to rounding off a day at the beach with a lightly chilled Millton Organic Gisborne Chardonnay.

Hawke's Bay

There are 75 vineyards in the Hawke's Bay region, and a bunch of superb restaurants and cafés. What more could you ask for? Gannets? Well, Hawke's Bay has those, too.

Cape Kidnappers 88 Fine Wine 90 Te Mata Peak 92

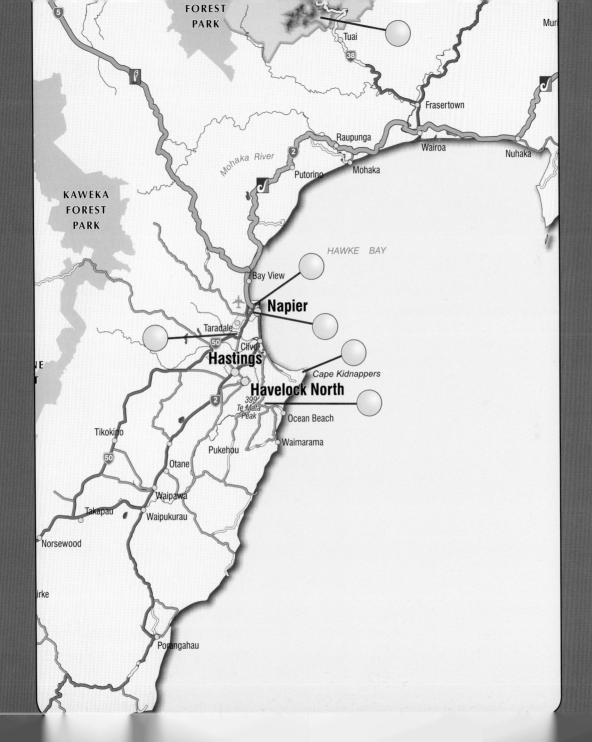

Cape Kidnappers

Captain Cook had plenty to say in his log about the southern headland of Hawke's Bay. After all, it was here that a party of Maori had tried to carry away one of the Tahitian passengers he had aboard. The boy was returned after the *Endeavour's* crew fired on the fleeing waka with cannon and musket and Cook named the headland Cape Kidnappers in honour of the incident.

Strangely, though, the observant Yorkshireman didn't say anything about gannets, even though Cape Kidnappers now hosts the world's largest and most accessible mainland colony of the big, yellow-headed birds. It's possible the colony wasn't there in Cook's time, as gannets prefer to nest on offshore rocks and islands and the Kidnappers colony had only 50 breeding pairs when first described in 1870. Now it has over 2200.

You can get to this ornithological marvel under your own steam, on foot, or you can join any one of a number of guided, motorised tours. In the most entertaining of these, you are seated aboard a large dray drawn by a tractor. In every case, the guides are adept at explaining the points of interest along the way, as well as the quirks of gannet behaviour.

The worst time to visit the colony is between May and mid-July, when the birds are all out at sea stocking up for the big breeding effort ahead. They begin returning to roost in July, and from August onward, the nesting sites on the high, humped spine of the Cape are a bustling, pungent, feathery furore. Gannet courting rituals, where the birds face each other, extend their long bills skyward and commence a kind of sword-fight, are the funniest mating behaviours you'll see outside Singles Night at the Red Rooster Tavern.

Full-grown gannets weigh two kilos — more than a size 14 chook — and have a wingspan of two metres. They're quite a sight wheeling in from the sea. Some of the birds arriving to get some action are last year's chicks which, incredible as it seems, took off from Kidnappers on their maiden flight as soon as they thought they could fly. Without the benefit of any kind of practice, guidance or experienced tuition, they then flew to Australia for their OE.

While you're in the Kidnappers area, there's plenty of other things to do. There's the brand-new, world-class golf course at the Cape itself, which commands spectacular views of Hawke's Bay. There's a bunch of museums in and around Haumoana and Te Awanga, including a petting zoo, a Clydesdale ranch where you can ride a cart behind draught horses, and a British car museum boasting the largest collection of Morris Minors in the world.

HAWKE'S BAY INCORPORATED

Cape Kidnappers hosts the world's largest and most accessible gannet colony but it isn't only for the birds.

Fine Wine

HAWKE'S BAY INCORPORATED

Abiding in the vines is an enjoyable way to spend the day.

There was a time when New Zealanders could get all the locally produced wine they wanted, so long as they got it from a handful of diehard Dalmatian winemakers making do with limited viticultural resources and licensing laws that viewed sales of wine to the general public as sly-grogging.

Ah, yes. Those were the days. When local wine was purchased from furtive gentlemen manning roadside stalls and served in restaurants in teapots. Those where the days when 'wining' was what we did about the weather, and dining was only ever done at home. We've come a wee way since then.

These days, much of the countryside that was once grazed by sheep is now turned over to chardonnay, semillon, cabernet and pinot noir. And our winemaking talent is footing it with the best in the world.

Need proof? There are a few regions you could head to, but in terms of getting the kind of broad sample of winemakers you need to make a really considered judgement, Hawke's Bay is the spot for you.

There are 75 vineyards in the area, and about half of them are happy to let the public in the cellar door. You can taste the fruits of their vines and their winemakers' zeal and, in many cases, have a bite to eat at the same time. Everyone but the hardest of hardcore sheep farmers will admit that vineyards are better to look at than sheep runs, and much nicer places to eat your lunch.

And that brings us to the other revolution that New Zealand has quietly undergone. Back in the 1980s, public opinion was divided on the merits or otherwise of Rogernomics. But few who endured the wilderness years of the New Zealand hospitality industry — the shall-we-go-Italian-or-Chinese years — will have had a word to say against what's happened to food in this country. We discovered there was life beyond carbonara and chop suey about the same time our Stalinist licensing laws were relaxed, so we learned 'haute cuisine' was not fancy French porridge about the same time we learned 'alfresco dining' was not a picture of the bloke who painted the Sistine Chapel tucking into his smoko.

So now you can sit outdoors at Havelock North's Black Barn, say, and choose (with difficulty) from several dozen New Zealand vintages to complement your fresh, locally grown, expertly prepared fare. And if you visit the Hawke's Bay farmers' market at the Hastings Showgrounds of a weekend, you can be sure there'll be more on offer than stringy hogget and prize swedes. Cheers, New Zealand.

FAVOURITES

BEST TRIP FOR FOODIES
Hawke's Bay Wine Country Food Trail

BEST FRESH STUFF
Hawke's Bay Farmers' Market, Tennyson Street, Napier and Kenilworth Road, Hastings

I LOVE YOU NEW ZEALAND

So much wine, so little time!
Samantha Taylor

HAWKE'S BAY INCORPORATED

Thousands of colourful grape vines now grace the Hawke's Bay landscape.

101 MUST-DO'S FOR KIWIS

Te Mata Peak

Hawke's Bay is laid out at the foot of Te Mata Peak.

The Maori legend about how Te Mata Peak in Hawke's Bay came to be, and why it so closely resembles the recumbent figure of a man is nearly as picturesque as the little town of Havelock North at the foot of the peak.

According to the legend, the local people of Heretaunga, fed up with being harassed by their neighbours, the people of the Waimarama region, held a council to decide what to do about it. Suffering from a military disadvantage, fighting was hardly an option. So it was clear an alternative means must be found.

The solution was proposed by an old kuia, who pointed to one of the tribe's more notable assets: the supreme beauty of the chief's daughter, Hinerakau. 'He ai na te wahine, ka horahia to po,' the old woman said: 'Womanly wiles will overcome the forces of darkness'.

Hinerakau obligingly placed herself at a point where the leader of the Waimarama raiders, a giant by the name of Te Mata o Rongokako, would see her, and he duly came, saw, and was conquered. Hinerakau then did as women do when they have a man completely in their power: she gave him some chores. Her affection, she admonished, would be indexed to his performance.

Te Mata took to his work with a will, easily accomplishing everything she set him to do. Until, that is, she invited him to chomp his way through the pesky range of hills that made access to the sea so tiresome for the people of the region.

Te Mata gave it a good crack — the deep gouge in the range known as The Gap is the bite he took out of it — but some part of this mouthful stuck in his craw, and he subsequently choked and died. He lies there still.

As for Hinerakau, she was so remorseful that she threw herself off a nearby cliff into the sea.

It's a mournful story, and one to contemplate as you enjoy the panoramic view from the 399 metre summit of Te Mata himself. On a clear day, you can see the whole of Hawke's Bay laid out before you, up to Mahia Peninsula in the north, and the rugged hills ranged behind the coast to the south. Inland, you'll see the snowy cap of Ruapehu glimmering, and at Te Mata's foot, you'll see the bounty of the fertile Hawke's Bay farms, orchards and vineyards grazing and growing before your eyes.

The giant Te Mata sleeps on as the grapes grow at the Black Bridge Estate Vineyard.

101 MUST-DO'S FOR KIWIS

Taranaki, Wanganui, Ruapehu & Taupo

The trail left by the mountain Taranaki, from the Central Plateau out to West Cape, when he fled the wrath of his stroppy volcanic colleague, Ruapehu, is better known as the Whanganui River, and there are attractions and activities strung right along its length. From the angler's paradise that is Lake Taupo, skiing and tramping in Tongariro and Egmont national parks, the peerless canoeing trip down the Whanganui itself and the derelict remains of the region's history to the refined pleasures of New Plymouth, it's all here.

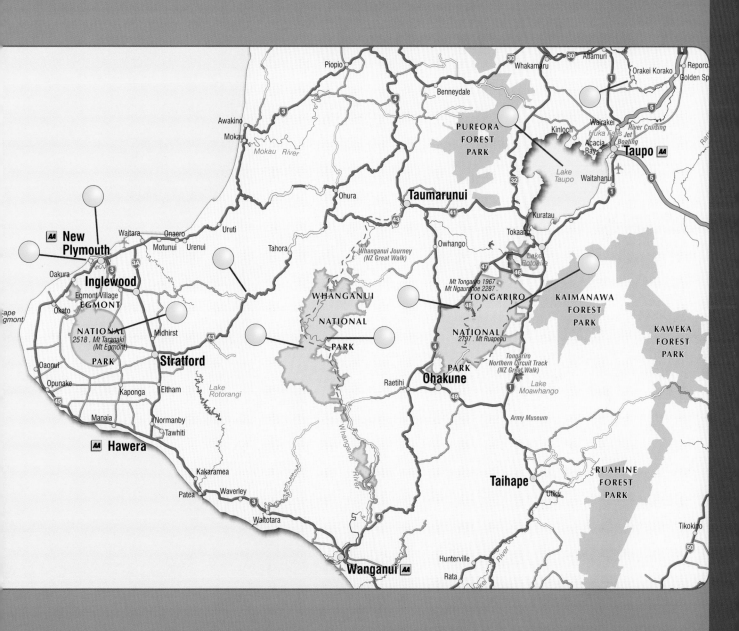

Lake Taupo's Top Water Attractions

The biggest lake in Australasia announced its arrival with a bang. Taupo is actually the drowned caldera of a super volcano, the eruption of which, in the first century AD, caused meteorological effects that were noted by sky-gazers as far afield as Rome and China. A layer of ash was deposited by the eruption the length and breadth of the nation — conveniently, as it happens, as this is used by geologists as a datum to judge the age of other rock and soil layers.

Over the centuries, the great hole in the earth torn by that cataclysmic event has filled with lovely, pure water, awaiting only the introduction of trout — browns from 1885, and rainbow a little later — to become an angler's paradise.

There are plenty of guides who will show you the best spots and let you in on the secrets du jour; you can hire a boat and a skipper, or you can try your own luck. The fishing in the lake, and in the rivers and streams feeding and emptying it — particularly the Waikato and the world-famous Tongariro — is rated among the best in the world, with trophy fish landed regularly. You can fish with a licence year round, and whether fly-casting, spinning or harling from the shore or trolling from a boat, with a little due deference to local knowledge, you'll be in with a shot. It's always a thrill to get a fish on the line, especially here: Taupo trout don't muck about when they're hooked up.

You can't buy wild trout, so the only

Australasia's biggest lake is the perfect place to chill out.

FAVOURITES

BEST PRAWNS
Huka Prawn Park, Huka Falls Road, Wairakei Park

BEST ADRENALINE RUSH
Taupo Bungy, Spa Rd

BEST COFFEE
Zest Café, Rifle Range Rd

DESTINATION LAKE TAUPO

way you'll get to eat one is to catch it yourself. Restaurants are permitted to cook them for you, but perhaps the best way to enjoy your catch is to have it smoked and take it away with you.

If fishing's not your thing, there's plenty to do besides in the vicinity of Taupo. There's boating or water-skiing on the lake. There are the geothermal curiosities of Wairakei and, of course, the impressive Huka Falls. Just beyond the point where

Lake Taupo empties into the North Island's largest river, the Waikato, the flow is funnelled into a narrow rocky gorge, through which it thunders at a rate of 200,000 litres per second. There's a walkway across the river at the top of the falls that leads to a platform at the base, from which the view — and the photo opportunity — is massive. You'll struggle for words to describe the falls, but that's okay: no one would be able to hear them, anyway.

Lake Taupo also offers adrenaline rushes for the thrill-seeker.

HUKAFALLS JET

101 MUST-DO'S FOR KIWIS

Mount Taranaki

Mount Taranaki keeps a watchful eye on Cape Egmont.

You want a nice, classically shaped volcano? Well, look no further. Along with Japan's Mount Fujiyama, Taranaki is about as close as you can get to the ideal of volcanic beauty — almost perfectly round — its nearly perfectly symmetrical cone rising to a pointed summit, with a single crater. Indeed, Taranaki so closely resembles Fuji that the film *The Last Samurai*, set in Japan and starring Tom Cruise, featured Taranaki as Fuji's stunt double. And it could be said that our maunga made a far better fist of his role than Cruise did.

The boundary of Egmont National Park

VENTURE TARANAKI/ROB TUCKER

was created by literally scribing a circle on the map with its centre on the mountain's summit. Seen from above, the dark green of the beech forest on the mountain's lower slopes is sharply defined against the lighter green of the surrounding dairy country.

Taranaki is an ancestor, a source of mana and a protective influence for the local iwi, and it's easy to see why they feel that way. Wherever you are in the Taranaki region, the mountain rises serenely on the horizon.

There's a skifield high on the slopes of Mount Taranaki, where you can go boarding and skiing. And Taranaki is reputed to be New Zealand's most-climbed mountain. It's a steady eight- or nine-hour haul to the summit, depending on your fitness, the conditions and which side you tackle it from. There's no special difficulty involved beyond the usual rigours of alpine ascents, and even the snow and ice are negotiable without specialised equipment in summer.

Why, then, does Taranaki see-saw in the stakes with Aoraki/Mount Cook as our deadliest peak? It's because the mountain is playing Kate Winslet to the North Island's Titanic, perched prettily there on the bow of the land as it ploughs into some fairly turbulent weather systems. Mountain weather always changes quickly: Taranaki's mood swings are as dramatic as they can be deadly. But with the relevant precautions observed, it's a terrific climb, and the views from the summit are gorgeous.

There are few places in the world where you can round off a day's mountaineering with an hour's surfing in a swell turned to amber glass by the setting sun. Well, here you can. The 105 kilometre road south

from New Plymouth around Cape Egmont has been cannily designated the Surf Highway. There are several top-class breaks along here, such as the Kumara Patch, Stent Road, Weld Road and the evocatively named Graveyards.

Take the road to Taranaki.

VENTURE TARANAKI/JOSH WOSKETT

New Plymouth's Coastal Walkway

New Plymouth started life as a port servicing the mellow, fertile dairying country surrounding Mount Taranaki. Not that there was any kind of natural harbour there, but compared with the rest of the inhospitable weather-edge of the central North Island, the comparative shelter offered by the Sugar Loaves — the set of little islets just offshore — was a natural choice.

Besides dairying, New Plymouth has become the centre of New Zealand's indigenous petrochemical industry, such as it is. Crude oil was first discovered at Moturoa Beach in 1865, where locals had long noted an oily ooze wherever they kicked rocks aside on the foreshore. Over the next 100 years, oil was sporadically extracted from the ground and sold locally under the brand Peak Petroleum, the advertising featuring a likeness of Mount Taranaki.

By the time crude production had petered out in 1972, interest had shifted offshore into the North and South Taranaki Bights, which are now dotted with drilling rigs tapping substantial natural gas and condensate reserves far below the sea floor. Just north of the city, one plant synthesises petrol from natural gas, and another manufactures methanol.

On the back of these two industries, New Plymouth has grown into a funky little city. The view from just about everywhere is dominated by Taranaki's paternal presence. And the heart of town is graced by the beautiful Pukekura Park, which hosts the annual WOMAD (World of Music and Dance) Festival, attracting indigenous and folk musicians from around the globe.

The formerly bleak, windswept black sands of the city's foreshore have lately

Len Lye's Wind Wand waves welcome.

VENTURE TARANAKI/JANE DOVE JUNEAU

been extensively developed into a walkway, with a number of points of interest dotted along its seven-kilometre length. Starting from the eastern or golf club end, you'll have access, should you choose to avail yourself of the opportunity, to the surf beaches at Fitzroy and East End. On the central section of the walkway in front of the city, you can admire the most distinctive of New Plymouth's many pieces of public art — the 45 metre Wind Wand, a kinetic contraption designed by internationally noted sculptor Len Lye to bend before the wind, of which there is seldom a shortage.

Here, too, are the city's famous Puke Ariki museum, library and visitors' centre — named for the pa that stood near this site in pre-European times — and the excellent Govett-Brewster Art Gallery.

Inland from these amenities are cafés, restaurants and bars, and a seven-kilometre walk is easily enough to make you feel you've earned a cold one. The walkway continues on to terminate at the port.

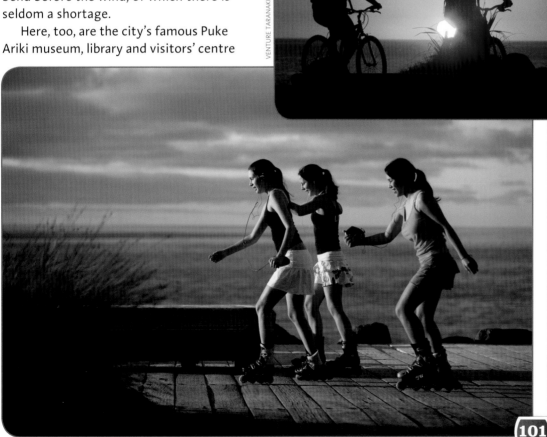

VENTURE TARANAKI/ROB TUCKER

VENTURE TARANAKI/ROB TUCKER

Walkers, mountain bikers and skaters all regularly use the coastal walkway.

Orakei Korako

There are still reminders scattered about the Taupo district of the subterranean forces that produced its mighty first-century eruption and subsequent lake. There are several hot-spots around the lake itself, where hot water surprises the wader in the ice-cold lake. The hillside above the little Maori village of Waihi steams and fumes, and the bathing pools at both Tokaanu and Taupo township's Royal Armed Constabulary Baths are hydrothermally heated.

Indeed, the main attraction for visitors to Lake Taupo as late as the 1920s was the thermal resort at Wairakei, reached by a long, bum-numbing ride over awful roads slung on the primitive suspension of the early cars.

Just 25 minutes north of Taupo on State Highway 1, if the wind's in the right direction and you've got the windows down, you'll catch a whiff of sulphur shortly before you see the turnoff to yet another geothermal site, Orakei Korako. It's tempting just to keep on driving, but if you do, you'll have missed out on the best geothermal park in New Zealand — one that's perversely better known to overseas visitors than it is to Kiwis.

From the park's entrance, where there is a café and an observation area, you take a ferry across Lake Ohakuri to where the geothermal action is. The landscape is fabulously coloured, stained by all the minerals deposited by the water bubbling up from the depths of the earth. The Maori name means something along the lines of 'painted place', and it's easy to see why.

Unlike most of our other thermal areas, Orakei Korako has never been mined, extensively developed or otherwise exploited, so it's as close to its pristine state as you could ask. For this reason, and because it's like a little slice of the Jurassic Age in the here and now, it was filmed by the BBC as a backdrop for their recent television series, *Walking with Dinosaurs*.

There are more active geysers here (35) than in any other geothermal field in New Zealand, along with a champion array of entertainingly obscene mud pools, fizzing hot springs, and furiously snorting fumaroles. There's also one of the largest silica terraces left in the world, after the destruction of the Pink and White Terraces in 1886, and a short bush walk leads to Ruatapu cave, where you can descend into the warm earth and reflect on (and in) the mirror-calm surface of an underwater pool.

PHOTO NEW ZEALAND/JEREMY BRIGHT

The Emerald
Terrace at
Orakei Korako.

101 MUST-DO'S FOR KIWIS

Ruapehu, Ngauruhoe & Tongariro

PHOTO NEW ZEALAND

Mount Ruapehu looks peaceful, but is prone to violent eruptions.

Donating the area that is now a national park to the people of New Zealand before the government could nick it was a masterstroke on the part of the paramount chief of Tuwharetoa, Te Heuheu Tukino IV, in 1887. The act guaranteed access to all New Zealanders for all time to one of the North Island's most interesting bits of landscape, and in kicking off the national parks system it also began the process of trying to preserve the land from the ravages of development and exploitation.

Fittingly, of the several peaks of Mount Ruapehu, the one that bears Te Heuheu's name is second only to the tipuna, 2,797 metre Ruapehu himself.

The drive around Ruapehu and his neighbours, Tongariro and Ngauruhoe, is spectacular enough at any time of year. But those who content themselves with the view from the window are missing out, because there's so much to be done beyond the reach of motor cars.

In the winter, there's skiing and

snowboarding, of course. Whakapapa, Turoa and Tukino skifields offer a superb variety of terrain, with a comparatively reliable season extending from the end of June to October, sometimes even longer.

Even in the summer, the skifields are worth a visit. The main chairlift at Whakapapa is generally open for sightseeing, and there's a café at the top. Those who wish can proceed higher up the mountain — it's a relatively short scramble from the top of the Knoll Ridge to the mountain's summit plateau. Guided walks are conducted to the crater lake — the sullen-looking, milky waters steaming away to remind visitors that this is an active volcano, and not to be trifled with.

Ruapehu has blown its top in major fashion several times in recent memory, with a violent ash eruption in 1945 and another burst of activity in 1995 and 1996. Its most deadly display, on Christmas Eve of 1953, was one of its least spectacular. A rise in the lake level saw the crater wall breached and a lahar — a landslide of volcanic mud and debris — swept away a rail bridge just in time for the Auckland–Wellington service to happen along and plunge into the river, at a cost of 151 lives. Another lahar is imminent today: that thought will liven things up as you drive through the automatic floodgates intersecting the round-the-mountain road.

There's plenty of tramping in the area, including the Tongariro Crossing, Ruapehu's classic round-the-mountain track, and lots of day walks, too. Or there's the high life at the Chateau Tongariro — even a round of golf at New Zealand's most elevated nine-hole course.

I LOVE YOU NEW ZEALAND

The Waiouru Army Museum and Tokaanu hot pools are worth a visit when the ski slopes are closed.
Anne Bennett

PHOTO NEW ZEALAND/GEOFF MARSHALL

The perfect cone of Mount Ngauruhoe rises above the Desert Road.

Taranaki Gardens

VENTURE TARANAKI/ROB TUCKER

Ostler's Garden in
East Stratford.

Where, asks an old song, have all the flowers gone? Well, you'd be forgiven for thinking Taranaki had got the lot if you did a tour of the gardens of the region between spring and autumn.

Taranaki hosts an annual Rhododendron and Garden Festival, and it's hard to miss the fact that these brilliantly coloured and widely varied shrubs have taken to the fertile, volcanic soils in the shadow of Mount Taranaki. One of the best places to see them in full, riotous bloom is the huge Pukeiti rhododendron garden just south of New Plymouth, set like a jewel in 320 hectares of rainforest. There are over 10,000 varieties there, and they compete vigorously for visitors' attention every year between July and Christmas.

The art of laying out and maintaining a traditional English garden has been perfected at Tikorangi, a property that has been carefully cultivated and tended by four generations of the Jury family. At the other extreme, Te Kainga Marire is one of New Zealand's finest urban native gardens, and it has been developed in such a way as to highlight the historical and cultural significance of its site.

In the heart of New Plymouth itself, a two-hour stroll through the large, informal public garden in Pukekura Park is one of the city's highlights. Laid out in 1876, it features some spectacular, mature specimen trees, and pathways meander through thickets of native and exotic plantings and past ponds and fountains. The biennial WOMAD Festival and annual summer concert series are held in Pukekura Park's bowl — an earthen amphitheatre.

A little further afield, there's the Hollard Gardens at Manaia, featuring a heritage plant collection. Ngamamaku at Oakura, at the very foot of Mount Taranaki and on the border of Egmont National Park, is noted for the boardwalk that bears visitors into a fern- and nikau-filled valley. And for a fine collection of exotic deciduous, broadleaf and coniferous trees, you'll want to drop in on Te Popo Gardens in Stratford.

All in all, there are 47 gardens in the Taranaki area that are open to the public, and 15 of these are considered to have national or regional significance. They're a sight to make the heart glad — especially since you don't have to do the weeding.

I LOVE YOU NEW ZEALAND

The festival of lights is on at the end of December to early February. In Pukekura Park, the fountain and waterfall are lit up at night, not to mention the lakes, trees etc. It is a wonderful event and is free.
Trish Keen

Discovering any of Taranaki's 47 public gardens is a must-do.

VENTURE TARANAKI/ROB TUCKER

The Bridge to Nowhere

Politicians have got a lot to answer for. In 1919, the government decided to allot land to diggers who had returned from the First World War battlefields, as a way of getting them restarted on civvy street. One of the areas it chose for this was the Mangapurua Valley in the rugged, virgin-bush-clad interior of the lower North Island, handy to the Whanganui River.

Forty families were packed off there. As the returned soldiers, their families and their possessions travelled upriver by boat, the gloomy bush crowding to the banks on either side, they must have wondered what the hell they were doing. Good question.

The men toiled to clear their 450 hectare holdings, using axes, saws, fire and sheer hard work. The women set up a school in an abandoned house, and everyone got on with trying to live a normal life.

For a time, as pasture took root in the soil made fertile by the ashes of the rainforest, there was a glimmer of hope. But stock failed to thrive and prices fell. It turned out the soil was as devoid of essential trace elements as the Mangapurua settlement concept was empty of sense, and once the dump of nutrients from the burnoff had been depleted, the land was worse than marginal.

The government persisted in its misguided attempts to improve the lot of its returned soldiers. Mindful of the access difficulties, with rain and rockfall frequently blocking the shingle tracks and carrying away the makeshift suspension bridge the settlers used to reach Raetihi, the government ordered the construction of a proper road, complete with a new concrete bridge.

By the time construction was completed in 1936, however, the Depression had bitten deep, and only three tenacious families clung on at Mangapurua. The rest had simply walked off their farms, leaving the bush to reclaim the remnants of their houses, land and dreams of prosperity.

Yet another flood damaged the road in 1942, and the government refused to patch it up. Instead, it evicted the last three families, giving them a paltry £250 apiece in compensation. The road disappeared in the bush, and grasses and lichens soon colonised the span and the deck of the bridge.

And there it stands today, an incongruous reminder in the middle of the bush of the madness of the plan and the misery of its executors. It's a pretty 40-minute walk from Mangapurua Landing on the Whanganui, or easily integrated into a two-day traverse of the Mangapurua track.

It's the grandest bridge on a tramping track you'll ever see.

PHOTO NEW ZEALAND

I LOVE YOU NEW ZEALAND

This is an awesome place to visit. Catch the Bridge to Nowhere jet boat from Pipiriki and travel up the Whanganui River to the Mangapurua Landing then walk to the bridge itself. A real remote wilderness area, like stepping back in time.
Amanda Jackson

Ponder the futility of the government's plans to resettle soldiers at the Bridge to Nowhere.

The Forgotten World Highway

Here's a word to the wise: if your fuel gauge is anywhere much below halfway by the time you reach Stratford, give serious thought to filling up. And if you're still thinking by the time you reach Toko: stop. Toko is the last sniff of gas you'll get on State Highway 43 until you reach Taumarunui, 150 kilometres distant. After all, it's not called the Forgotten World Highway for nothing: it's not as though there's traffic jams or anything.

What there are, instead, are the remnants of several settlements and townships that had their day in the sun along here while the Stratford–Okahukura railway line was being built. Long since abandoned, these are today just sites of historic interest on the map of New Zealand's first heritage trail.

The road took 50 years to complete until it was opened in 1945. There's some extraordinary scenery along here — some of the most unspoiled bush to be seen on any New Zealand roadside. The sheer walls of the Tarangakau Gorge, soar to 500 metres on either side, to say nothing of the peaks of Taranaki, Ruapehu, Ngauruhoe and Tongariro floating intermittently into view.

There's the 180 metre long, single-lane Moki tunnel, and a short side-trip and a brisk walk will bring you to the lovely Mount Dampier falls.

Around the halfway mark, you'll haul into Whangamomona. Overseas visitors to New Zealand often cherish its left-behind feel, but even the most dedicated nostalgia-hunter might think Whangamomona has taken this to extremes. It's hardly changed since the 1920s, and its residents have made a virtue of necessity. Whangamomona's one of the North Island's remotest townships — so remote, in fact, that the townspeople declared it a republic in 1988. The people of the district still celebrate Republic Day (15 January) every year, with a festival involving a kind of rustic Olympics of gumboot-throwing, possum skinning, whip-cracking and a Wild West shootout. To take part, and to be sure they'll let you through town unmolested, you'll need to apply for a passport, which you can do at the New Zealand embassy, alias 'The Whanga', the Whangamomona tavern.

It's a trip back in time.

I LOVE YOU NEW ZEALAND

Absolutely fabulous — I always take any overseas visitors or friends on this road if they haven't already been! The locals are fantastic and always very friendly. Plus the Whanga pub is great for a stopover!
Shannon Cox

Apply for a passport at the Whangamomona Hotel.

101 MUST-DO'S FOR KIWIS

Tongariro Crossing

Whereas many people's experience of the wonders of Tongariro National Park are limited to vistas of the volcanic peaks from the Desert Road or to a visit to the Mount Ruapehu skifields, the Tongariro Crossing offers those who take the trouble an insight into just why the park is rated an international treasure and listed as a World Heritage site.

The crossing takes seven or eight hours to complete at a steady pace and in favourable conditions. The total distance is 17 kilometres. It requires only a moderate level of fitness — although there are two points where the going can get pretty tough — but the reward is a day spent in some of the most extraordinary landscape New Zealand has to offer.

Most trampers tackle it from the western end, following the Mangatepopo Stream up to the foot of a steep saddle between Mount Tongariro and Mount Ngauruhoe.

You'll be puffing a bit by the time you reach the top of the Mangatepopo Saddle, but reaching the crest is like stepping onto the surface of another planet. The great, even-sided cinder cone of Ngauruhoe presides over an otherworldly scene of volcanic desolation — the ashen expanse of Tongariro's South Crater.

The route crosses to the far wall of South Crater and there's another brisk climb to the highest point on the crossing.

On a clear day, the views are breathtaking — over Lake Rotoaira to Lake Taupo or, in the other direction, across the North Island's rugged heartland to Mount Taranaki, 140 kilometres away.

The track now descends alongside Tongariro's Red Crater, with its mineral-stained walls and active fumaroles, and past the cluster of tarns known as the Emerald Lakes for their vivid, mineral-stained green water.

The track crosses Tongariro's Central Crater and passes Blue Lake before winding down a steep-walled valley. This opens out to a spectacular view of the volcanic hinterland, and the track meanders down the tussock slope to Ketetahi Hut.

For a time, the descent from the hut follows the course of the Ketetahi Stream, which is fed from a thermal spring higher up the mountainside. Beneath the snow-line, the final section of the track passes through beech forest in which native birds abound.

Most local accommodation providers offer transport to and from the Mangatepopo and Ketetahi ends of the track, and guides are available who can enhance the crossing experience by explaining the cultural, mythical, historical and natural significance of the landscape.

PHOTO: NEW ZEALAND/TONY BRUNT

I LOVE YOU NEW ZEALAND

Tongariro Crossing is very beautiful — equally stunning is the track to Tama Lakes from Whakapapa. It gives you a real appreciation of why (rightly so!) we are called the most beautiful country in the world.
Neill Sperath

The Emerald Lakes offer a stunning spot for a bit of a rest.

113

101 MUST-DO'S FOR KIWIS

Whanganui National Park

The Great Walk known as the Whanganui Journey sounds like one for the Lord. After all, Jesus is the only person who is said to have been equipped to walk it, given the Whanganui Journey is actually over water.

It follows a 145 kilometre section of the Whanganui River, from Taumaranui to Pipiriki, and everyone but the divine will accomplish it by watercraft. For over half of its course, there is no road access at all.

The 329 kilometre Whanganui is New Zealand's second-longest river and the largest navigable one. It was once the principal means of communication between the rugged interior of the North Island and the west coast, and Maori used it to trade goods down to the seaport of Wanganui.

Because of the difficulty of access, much of the land adjacent to the Whanganui was never logged or cleared, and so the drift downriver is through tracts of some of the most majestic rainforest remaining in the North Island. The canopy is populated with profuse birdlife, and your companions on the trip will be tui, fantail, kereru and, by night, you'll hear the shrill cries of kiwi.

Most who accomplish the Whanganui Journey do so in a Canadian-style canoe, which enables them to take more than the bare minimum of gear. Kayakers can share the pleasure, if they travel light. There are huts and campsites along the way, and a Great Walks pass will entitle you to use them for six nights and seven days from the time of purchase — plenty of time to meander down the stream.

Of course, there's no obligation to haul out at Pipiriki. There's plenty of river left beyond that point, and those who venture further will find themselves shaking their heads and blinking at the placenames on their map: London, Corinth,

Athens and Jerusalem all drift by. These little townships, each with a picturesque marae and church, were renamed by early missionaries to the area, and are steeped in history. Hiruharama — Jerusalem — is the best known, as it was here that poet James K. Baxter chose to found a community for the down-and-out and disaffected; the white boulder, dragged from the Whanganui itself, that marks his grave is a rewarding pilgrimage.

A little lower down the river at Matahiwi — just south of London — there's the restored remains of a flour mill constructed by local Maori in the entrepreneurial days that followed European settlement.

Of course, if time presses, and you don't mind watching it all in fast-forward, you can always do the journey at high speed in a jetboat.

Take a canoe trip on the Whanganui River.

PHOTO NEW ZEALAND/IAN TRAFFORD

101 MUST-DO'S FOR KIWIS

Manawatu, Kapiti & Wairarapa

There's a variety of reasons to visit the lower half of the North Island. From the closest thing New Zealand has to a religious shrine, the Rugby Museum at Palmerston North, to a working model of Stonehenge; from the rugged, moody Castlepoint and Cape Palliser to the rainforest and profuse birdlife of Kapiti Island — you're spoiled for choice.

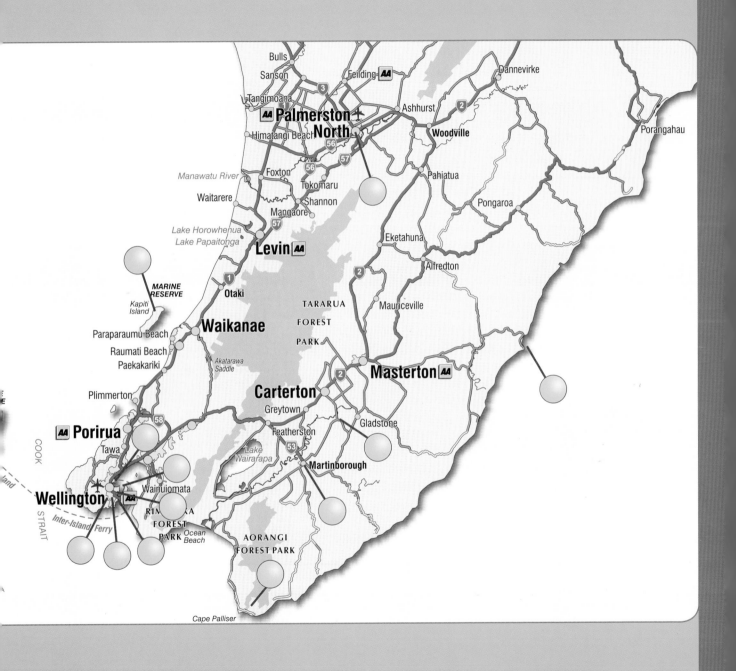

Cape Palliser

When a wind whips up from Antarctica and heads north driving a swell before it, the first bit of the North Island it hits is Cape Palliser. And like every other spot where land and sea come to serious blows, the cape is magic.

James Cook named Cape Palliser for a naval buddy of his, and the name was transferred to the great sweep of bay between the cape itself and Turakirae Head in the west.

The rugged coast is well-endowed with kai moana, so was an important spot for Maori. For the European sheep farmers who came next, driving their flocks around the coast from the Wainuiomata Valley, Palliser Bay was their gateway to the Wairarapa plains. And the beach, windswept and turbulent as it is, was the main point of lading for their produce, with wool bales lightered out to waiting ships by hard men leaning on the oars of surfboats.

Equally hard men — and leathery bach-owners — populate Palliser Bay today. Humble fibrolite buildings are dotted along its length, and at the little settlement of Ngawi, five kilometres from Cape Palliser itself, commercial fishermen draw their boats up on the steep, stony beach using old bulldozers and deft seamanship.

Perched on a promontory above the cape there's a lighthouse, which is worth the climb — no fewer than 250 steps, straight up — for the view it gives over the Bay and across Cook Strait to the South

I LOVE YOU NEW ZEALAND

Watch out where you drive as the seals are everywhere . . . You *must* climb the steps to the lighthouse and enjoy the Pacific Ocean rolling in below. Also stop and check out the tractors on the beach at Ngawi, the lovely fishing village just down the road. Patricia Hammond

Island in the misty distance. The highest point in the Inland Kaikoura range, snow-capped Tapuaeouenuku, is visible in all but the murkiest weather.

There's plenty to do in the area, ranging from fishing — whether aboard a chartered launch out of Ngawi or casting from the beach, whitebaiting at the egress of Lake Onoke in season, or diving for crayfish — to surfing or simply knocking about in a rented bach.

A few minutes back from Ngawi, there's a spectacular rock formation reached by an easy walk from the roadway, where the sedimentary limestone of this coast has been weathered into a set of soaring, fluted columns known as the Putangirua Pinnacles. That's well worth a look.

And of course, you could do worse than use your accommodation in Palliser Bay as a base from which to explore the vineyards, art galleries, museums and other attractions of the Wairarapa.

PHOTO NEW ZEALAND/MIKE HEYDON

The romantic 'Honeymoon Suite' looking out over Cook Strait.

Castle Point

Many of New Zealand's special coastal spots are marked by lighthouses. Castle Point is no exception. Named because the rock formation on the skyline above resembles — surprise, surprise — a castle when viewed from sea, it's one of the wilder stretches of the North Island coast.

The lighthouse is erected on a low, rocky islet that is intermittently connected to the mainland by a causeway of sand, depending on prevailing wind and tidal conditions. A wooden causeway forms more reliable access and the scramble up to the lighthouse, and around the weathered sedimentary rock of the islet itself, is well worth tackling. On a good day, you'll get a matchless view of the sunrise from here.

Inside the barrier formed by the rocks, there's a lagoon and a fine, hard, flat sandy beach, used for the Castlepoint Beach Races which happen every March — in theory, at least, as for each of the last few years a spell of easterly weather has arrived with tiresome bad timing to strip the sand from the beach and expose the rocks.

The lagoon is a popular swimming spot with day-trippers and those lucky enough to have access to a bach in the little settlement at Castlepoint. It's also the boat harbour for the local fishing fleet, for whom each excursion necessitates a complex ballet of seamanship and bulldozer driving. The swell washes incoming boats through the gap between the headland and the island (dubbed 'The Gap' by

I LOVE YOU NEW ZEALAND

My favourite local beach since I was knee high to a tuatara! A smorgasbord of awesome natural features. Lots of fond memories and safe swimming for the kids.
Anthony Carter

men with more on their minds than fancy, romantic sobriquets) like a cork from a bottle. As the skipper works his engines in the tricky tidal maelstrom, a crewman leaps onto the island and jogs around to fetch the bulldozer and trailer. Then, judging his moment, the skipper drives the boat onto the trailer, the dozer driver guns the machine up the beach and boat, crew and catch are all safe ashore.

Of course, if you feel the urge to watch this process up close, you can always sign on for a fishing charter. One benefit of working so inhospitable a coast is that the fishery is comparatively unspoiled, and angling fortune certainly favours those brave enough to ply these waters.

The stretch of beach opposite The Gap receives a hefty swell which is surfable in the right conditions. And even if the weather cuts up rough, there's the walk in the nearby scenic reserve to Castle Rock itself (you can view a little yellow daisy unique to this area on the way, in late summer), and the booming spray on the rocks to keep you entertained.

PHOTO NEW ZEALAND/MIKE HEYDON

Castle Point lighthouse is a popular day-trip for Wairarapa residents.

121

101 MUST-DO'S FOR KIWIS

Kapiti Island

If you have anything resembling a soft spot for the native birdlife of this country — and what Kiwi doesn't — it'd break your heart to read the accounts of the early settlers in the Wellington region. The first Europeans to camp at Petone actually took to rowing out to the ships at night, because the dawn chorus ashore was too loud. And kereru — the great, ungainly native wood pigeon — hung out in flocks thousands strong, crashing and whirring in the treetops.

In the 160-odd years since those descriptions were written, habitat destruction and introduced predators have ensured that the only parts of the North Island where you can catch a faint echo of the riotous heyday of New Zealand's songbirds are the bird sanctuaries such as Tiritiri Matangi in the Hauraki Gulf, the onshore 'island' of the Karori Wildlife Sanctuary in Wellington and Kapiti Island.

Of all of them, Kapiti is the most impressive. Lying only 60 minutes north of Wellington by road and then 15 minutes off Paraparaumu by launch, it's New Zealand's most accessible offshore wildlife sanctuary.

The island is an attractive destination in its own right. Stretching nearly ten kilometres and covering nearly 2000 hectares, its interior is rugged, elevated — the highest point is nearly 600 metres — and entirely clad in mature native bush.

Kapiti was the fortress of the formidable Ngati Toa rangatira, Te Rauparaha (author of the haka traditionally performed by the All Blacks), in the early days of European–Maori contact. Shore whaling stations came later, and parts of the island were farmed until 1897, when the government enacted legislation to create a wildlife reserve there.

Since a predator eradication programme in the 1980s completely removed rodents, mustelids and possums, several endangered bird species have been introduced or re-established on Kapiti Island. Here you can hear the fizz of the stitchbird, the fluting of the kokako, the shriek of the brown and little spotted kiwis, the chatter of the saddleback, all in addition to the ubiquitous honking of tuis, chiming of bellbirds and twittering of fantails.

You'll need to keep a weather eye on your lunch to protect it from the aerial assaults of kaka and stealthy ground incursions by weka, but this can be hard to do when you're trying to keep track of all the comings and goings in the canopy.

The sea around Kapiti Island is a marine reserve, and the profusion of aquatic species mirrors that of the birdlife. Onshore from here, there's the Waikanae Estuary Scientific Reserve, so that the area offers a complete experience of the recovering habitat.

Only 50 people may visit Kapiti at any one time, so when you do make the trip, you'll justly feel like one of the privileged few.

I LOVE YOU NEW ZEALAND

Kapiti's a great place, but don't just be satisfied with walking on it — talk to the boat operators about a cruise right around, and perhaps landing on the northern tip.
Frank Hogg

View Kapiti Island from Otaki Beach.

123

New Zealand Rugby Museum

Pompallier tried hard with Roman Catholicism. Marsden had a go with Anglicanism. Cargill and Burns did their level best with Presbyterianism. Missionaries of all stamps have come and gone throughout our history, and most have left their mark. But there is only one true religion round here, mate, and that's rugby union.

Our national Road-to-Damascus experience took place in 1905, when a touring party of footballers from this uttermost corner of the Empire arrived in the Old Country and proceeded to cut a swathe through England, Ireland, Scotland and Wales, taking time at the end of the British leg of the tour to evangelise France and North America with the union gospel too.

As they marched triumphantly from match to match, winning everything (but one game, of which we were robbed by a dodgy referee) and trampling the pride of British manhood underfoot, New Zealanders began sitting up and taking notice. Certainly the politicians noticed, and the Premier, Richard Seddon, became the first in a long line of New Zealand leaders to nail their political colours to the mast of the national rugby team.

That team was subsequently labelled 'the Originals', because not only were they the first truly representative national footy side to tour England, they were also the first to be called 'the All Blacks', on account of their black uniform.

You can find out all about the exploits of the Originals, of all the teams that came afterwards, and of the infancy of the code in this country — everything you ever wanted to know about footy, from the time of the first game played in Nelson in 1870 to the present — at the New Zealand Rugby Museum on Cuba Street in Palmerston North.

It's a small, unprepossessing building, but it contains a wealth of riches for the footy fanatic and the merely curious alike. The emergence of New Zealand as the world's major rugby power is set out in a fascinating collection of memorabilia, photos and artefacts, arranged in 30 displays by topic. There's also a library and archive, where practically everything ever

The New Zealand Rugby Museum.

NEW ZEALAND RUGBY MUSEUM

NEW ZEALAND RUGBY MUSEUM

published on the subject reposes, and where an impressive collection of primary records — players' tour diaries, newspaper cuttings and scrapbooks — makes the museum a mecca for sportswriters and researchers.

Museum founder and director Bob Luxford and his staff — bless them — are on hand to answer your questions, and group tours can be arranged on request. For anyone with a healthy respect for the oval ball, or a burning desire to know where that respect comes from, this is the place for you.

The Rugby Museum contains a wealth of riches for any footie fanatic.

Stonehenge Aotearoa

There used to be henges all over the ancient world. You probably could barely move about the countryside without falling over woodhenges, strawhenges, henges made of mud. For reasons of its durable construction, though, it is Stonehenge, on Salisbury Plain in England, that has survived, and even then, it's only partial — a few standing stones.

The modern world has leapt to all kinds of conclusions about its purpose, most of them involving aliens. But astronomers have always known better. They say Stonehenge was carefully laid out by the ancients to mark the movements of stars and planets, which were key indicators of the wheeling of the seasons. It is thus one of the first computers — a machine constructed to make sense of the universe.

To illustrate how henges work, and to teach New Zealanders about the patterns observable in our own heavens, a team of astronomers led by Richard Hall have constructed a henge in the Wairarapa, which opened for visits by the public in February 2005.

Superficially, it may resemble a reconstruction of the Salisbury Plains ruin — it's a circle of massive standing stones, capped with more stones — but it has been carefully tailored to the southern skies.

The stones have been placed to mark the rising of the sun, the moon, bright stars and certain constellations. There is also a 'star compass' that mirrors the vast rote knowledge of celestial comings-and-goings that enabled the ancestors of the Polynesians to cross huge tracts of ocean.

As the guided tour and audiovisual presentations at Stonehenge Aotearoa illustrate, such knowledge of the heavens was an essential survival tool, and not just for those who went down to the sea in canoes. The patterns in the sky foretold seasonal changes, and told observers when to plant, to harvest, and when to count on doing nothing but rugging up and huddling round large fires telling tall stories.

And it turns out it's no coincidence that such stories told by the ancient Greeks and the Polynesians, for example, featured the exploits of gods, men and animals whose forms can be seen in the sky. Myths serve as mnemonics — shorthand for all that knowledge of what goes where and when overhead. Myth and legend are the software, if you like, that makes henges work.

A visit to Stonehenge Aotearoa will give you a window on the minds of our most distant ancestors. It's also a beautiful and faintly mystical experience, night or day, at any time of year.

STONEHENGE AOTEAROA © CHRISTOPHER PICKERING

Experience the beauty of evening at Stonehenge Aotearoa.

Wellington

Pace the corridors of power and see how you like it on a tour of Parliament Buildings. If, however, you're more interested in culture than politics, you can stroll Wellington's waterfront and ponder the Writers' Walk on your way to Te Papa Tongarewa, otherwise known as Our Place. Leave time to do all three before you embark on what has been called the prettiest ferry ride in the world, the Interislander service, for the South Island leg of your grand, must-do tour.

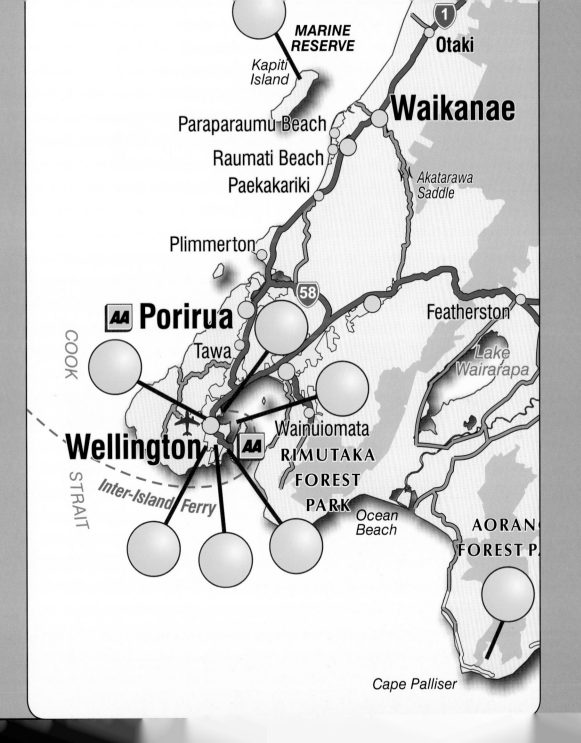

MARINE
RESERVE

*Kapiti
Island*

(1) Otaki

Waikanae

Paraparaumu Beach

Raumati Beach

Paekakariki

*Akatarawa
Saddle*

Plimmerton

58

Featherston

AA **Porirua**

Tawa

*Lake
Wairarapa*

COOK

Wellington

AA

Wainuiomata

Inter-Island Ferry

STRAIT

RIMUTAKA

FOREST

PARK

*Ocean
Beach*

AORAN
FOREST P

Cape Palliser

Te Papa Tongarewa

In the age of empty slogans, it's easy to dismiss the English paraphrase of the Maori name of Te Papa Tongarewa — 'Our Place' — as simply more marketing speak.

In fact, the Museum of New Zealand represents a state-of-the-international-art facility dedicated to showing New Zealanders the here-and-now, as well as the then-and-there, of our country. Te Papa is big — at 36,000 square metres, far too big to take in entirely on one visit — but if you don't have the time or opportunity to come back again and again, you can take a guided tour tailored to the ages and attention spans of your party.

There are rooms and exhibits specifically targeted at children, where they can get their hands on everything from clothes for dress-ups to tools and materials with which to invent things. That'll keep them happy while the adults marvel at Jeff Thompson's corrugated-iron tribute to the HQ Holden, the John Britten motorcycle, bits of Phar Lap, and one of Captain Cook's cannons.

Everyone leaves Te Papa with their own set of favourites. In the *Awesome Forces* room, you stand in the *Earthquake House* while a commentary prepares you for what's to come by recounting the events of a major 1987 earthquake as experienced by Edgecumbe residents. Then a dull roar starts, and the little building twists and shivers like a dog having a really bad dream. There are 121 such interactive exhibits in Te Papa.

The natural history of these islands is comprehensively covered. There are also moving and fascinating displays on the forces that shaped our human geography, too — the patterns of migration that brought and turned us all into the lucky, lucky inhabitants of the greatest little country on earth.

Another very popular exhibit is the animated junk shop and the 'Golden Days' video montage that it contains. The makers of the video must have blanched when they were asked to represent New Zealand's entire recorded history in twenty television minutes, but they've risen magnificently to the challenge. It's just one of 26 audiovisual exhibits.

The beautiful marae that takes pride of place on the top floor of the building celebrates our ethnic diversity while affirming New Zealand's biculturalism. The stained glass window is the jewel in the crown of the supreme architectural achievement that is the building itself, set as it is among reconstructed aspects of the New Zealand landscape, all merging stylishly with a lagoon and the rest of Wellington's waterfront.

It's a place we all should be proud to call our own.

Be sure to visit
'Our Place'.

101 MUST-DO'S
FOR KIWIS

The Beehive &
Parliament Buildings

By the standards of contemporary architecture, you might think Parliament House is pretty fancy. All that Takaka marble, the pillars, the columns and porticoes are hardly what you'd see on an architect's easel these days.

Amazingly, however, it's only half of what it would have been if the architect had got his way. The design is based on two different concepts submitted by John Campbell in 1911, placed first and fourth in a competition run by the Premier, Joseph Ward, for a design replacing the previous set of parliament buildings, which were burned down in 1907. Campbell's two designs were amalgamated into one great Edwardian, neocolonial extravagance with more urns, balustrades and cupolas than you could poke a Black Rod at.

The government baulked at the expense, however, and the half-a-parliament that fits between the old Parliamentary Library (which survived the fire) and the Beehive is the result.

The Beehive is reputed to have been sketched on a napkin by British architect Sir Basil Spence, who was consulted on the project in 1964 after the bickering and infighting among New Zealand's normally peace-loving community of architects threatened to slide into full-scale civil war.

The name, too, is supposed to have been just as ad hoc. Spence is said to have dug in his pocket and produced a box of Beehive matches, and the name stuck. To think, the seat of power in this country might well have been known as The Lighter or The PXT-Capable WAP Browser Phone if the same approach had been taken today.

Strolling the corridors of power makes for a fascinating tour. Besides the architectural features and (in the case of the Beehive) peculiarities, the commentary explains the political process in all its complexity. If the members aren't sitting that day, you can even pace about the Debating Chamber and sit in some member's chair, while you decide whether you're with the Ayes, the Noes or some other misspelled part of facial anatomy altogether.

If Parliament is in session, you can look on from the Public Gallery. The best time to do this is during Question Time, when the heavyweights are likely to be warming the front benches and engaging in the kind of refined and intellectual sparring you'll only ever see in the rarefied precincts of parliament — or at kindy after everyone's had a bit too much sugar.

I LOVE YOU NEW ZEALAND

The free tour is well worth your time. Very interesting even for those not interested in politics. It's great to be able to get in amongst the inner workings of your own country.
Nicola Elliott

Colonial extravagance meets 1960s style at New Zealand's Parliament Buildings.

The Interislander Experience

Anyone who has ever done a road trip of New Zealand will have indelible memories of their Cook Strait crossing.

The strait is a wild piece of water, where the great, oceanic currents sweeping up the west coast of the South Island funnel through the channel between Cape Terawhiti at the southwest tip of the North Island and Arapawa Island at the entrance to the South Island's Marlborough Sounds. The sea floor here, what's more, rises toward what was once a land bridge linking the islands, and the weather systems that march in from the west find themselves blocked by land to the north and south, with nowhere to go but straight through the strait.

For that reason, it's not at all uncommon to have a bumpy ride going across the strait. The Interislander service runs three road-rail ferries, and all three — the Kaitaki, the Arahura and the Aratere — are big, powerful ships. Yet they still feel the muscles of the strait when it chooses to flex them. Bumping through the swell, watching the land dimmed by squalls, is as close as most people get in this day and age to experiencing the rigours of

Kaitaki arrives in Wellington.

INTERISLANDER

the sea passage that brought many of our ancestors to these shores. It's exhilarating.

If you strike the strait on a day when it gets a little too exhilarating for your tastes, spare a thought for the passengers of the forerunner of the present Wellington–Picton service in the days before the South Island Main Trunk railway line connected Picton to Christchurch. The ferry between islands in those days was an overnight proposition between Wellington and Lyttleton, which a southerly buster could turn into a terrifying epic.

Even on a rough day, it's easy to see as you cruise the perpetually serene waterway of the sheltered Queen Charlotte Sound, why it is that the 92 kilometre, three-hour Interislander cruise has been described as one of the most beautiful in the world.

And you are, in any case, more than likely to find the strait in one of its benign moods, when the sights of the sounds and the rugged Wellington coast are rolled out before you for your viewing pleasure.

The facilities aboard all three vessels are first rate, with a range of highly palatable food and beer, wines and spirits available at the bar. There are entertainment amenities for young and old — especially the young — so more often than not it seems as though it's all over just a little too soon.

INTERISLANDER

it's not always a bumpy ride aboard the Arahura.

Wellington Writers' Walk

Wellington's waterfront is the envy not only of most other New Zealand cities, but also of many cities around the world. It's been developed in a way that maximises the city's location, crowded by the surrounding hills against the harbour. After all, it's far too nice a body of water to screen off behind container cranes and warehouses. The whole crescent from Chaffers Marina (where you'll find Te Papa Tongarewa and the magnificent, brand-new Waitangi Park) to Queens Wharf has been opened out, with a broad boulevard at the water's edge lined with bars, restaurants and public artworks.

The sculptures include a Len Lye kinetic piece, the Water Whirler, the eccentric and wonderful Wellington City to Sea Bridge, and a depiction of the discovery of Wellington Harbour by the Polynesian navigator, Kupe.

Winding around the waterfront is the innovative Wellington Writers' Walk, a series of concrete plaques bearing quotations from fifteen noted New Zealand writers who have or had strong links to Wellington. They range from the little-known — his plaque on the walk may be the only enduring memorial writer and journalist Pat Lawlor will have in New Zealand literature — to the giants: Katherine Mansfield, Robin Hyde, Bruce Mason, Maurice Gee and Patricia Grace all called the capital home at some time in their lives.

The Writers' Walk was the brainchild of the Wellington branch of the New Zealand Society of Authors, and the first stage was opened in 2001. Each plaque was cast to the direction of typographer Catherine Griffiths. The words are picked out in high relief, and in a tall, bold font. The sun casts the shadows of the words, making them stand out from their industrial concrete matrix.

THEN OUT OF THE TUNNEL AND WELLINGTON BURST LIKE A BOMB IT OPENED LIKE A FLOWER WAS LIT UP LIKE A ROOM, EXPLAINED ITSELF EXACTLY, BECAME THE CAPITAL.

ROBERT CATO/WWW.CATO.CO.NZ

Follow the Writers' Walk and experience the words of Denis Glover, Alistair Te Ariki Campbell and Maurice Gee.

BLUE RAIN FROM A CLEAR SKY, OUR WORLD A CUBE OF SUNLIGHT – BUT TO THE SOUTH THE VIOLET ADMONITION OF THUNDER.

ROBERT CATO/WWW.CATO.CO.NZ

The walk meanders from Chaffers Marina, to Frank Kitts Park and the City to Sea Bridge. You can either pick up a pamphlet that will guide you from plaque to plaque, or you can let them surprise you as you stroll along the waterfront.

The sites for all 15 were chosen so as to place the quotation in proximity to a view of Wellington and its harbour. Perhaps most striking of all is James K. Baxter's, which seems to float above the surface of the pool outside Te Papa, reflected in the water on the capital's rare windless days.

Each quotation is a perspective on the city, and invites you to meditate as you walk. Wellington 'bursts like a bomb', is 'the edge of the universe', 'a place where magic can be made and miracles occur', a 'dear city', where 'there is always an edge . . . requiring vigilance', and 'the world headquarters of the verb'.

Nelson

It's known as New Zealand's sunshine capital, and the geographical centre of the country is in Nelson, too. It's a major fishing port, and the centre of a thriving wine region. You'd expect the lifestyle around here to be pretty good, and you'd be right. It's also the gateway to some pretty special areas — the Kahurangi and the Abel Tasman national parks, Farewell Spit and Takaka.

Abel Tasman National Park

It may be the smallest national park in the country, but what it lacks in size, the Abel Tasman National Park sure makes up for in location.

The 22,530 hectare Abel Tasman National Park occupies the blunt headland that separates Tasman Bay from Golden Bay. Its name commemorates the visit here, in 1642, of Dutch navigator Abel Tasman: four of his crew members were killed in the first, inauspicious contact between Europeans and the Maori at their anchorage. Visitors will agree that Golden Bay is a far more pleasant title than that which Tasman gave it: Murderers' Bay.

Parts of the Abel Tasman National Park can be accessed by car, and it makes for a stunning scenic flight. But between the road-heads at Sandy Bay and Totaranui, its glories can only really be experienced on foot or by watercraft. This 50 kilometre stretch is a world-renowned kayaking location, not just because of the natural beauty of its hidden coves, rugged granite cliffs and unspoiled granite-crumb beaches, but also because of the diversity of its marine life, much of which is protected by the Tonga Island Marine Reserve.

Seal colonies are a regular sight for kayakers, and their residents will sometimes invite themselves along for the ride as you paddle around the coastline. Encounters with dolphins and penguins are common, too, and taking a mask and snorkel along is rewarding, thanks to the area's clear water and abundant fish life.

Gliding on the azure waters fringed by bush and blinding white-sand beaches, paddling in the shadow of the massive granite boulder known as Split Apple Rock — these are must-have Kiwi experiences.

For those who don't feel up to getting

about by paddle-power, however, there are timetabled water taxi services to some of the park's jewel-like bays, bringing them within reach for picnic parties of all ages and abilities.

For sworn land lubbers, there's the 51 kilometre Abel Tasman Walkway. The track is accessible at four points, making it ideal for day-trippers, but there are huts and campsites available for those doing the entire walk. This is justly listed as one of New Zealand's Great Walks, and alternating between a meandering path through the bush and crossing dazzling beaches, it takes three or four days to complete at a leisurely pace. The sun and swimming are at their best in the summer, but with the song of tui and bellbird to keep you company, walking the Abel Tasman is an unforgettable experience at any time of year.

Visit Split Apple Rock in a sea kayak or a waka.

LATITUDE NELSON

101 MUST-DO'S FOR KIWIS

Enjoy the Catch of the Day

Funnily enough, the original European residents of what came to be known as Nelson (after a certain admiral) didn't want to be there at all. They'd hoped to settle in Auckland, or Canterbury, or anywhere else in the new land where you could run stock. In the end, though, at the insistence of the government, the New Zealand Company — who were a cross between travel agents, employment consultants, real estate agents and wide boys — was obliged by government directive to found a town in what was then known as Blind Bay.

The site didn't have a hell of a lot going for it, but it did have a sheltered anchorage, tucked in behind a long boulder bank (in fact, at 13 kilometres, the longest in the southern hemisphere). As they grizzled about how poor the land was, they overlooked the potential of the magnificent terroir of the hinterland, the Waimea and Rai valleys, to produce world class wine grapes. And they failed to consider the bounty that was there in the sea.

Today, Nelson is the largest fishing port in Australasia, and Nelson Haven behind the Boulder Bank is home to a large and productive fleet of cray- and wet-fishing vessels, as well as the tenders of shellfish aquaculture.

You'd expect the kai moana to be pretty good in these parts and you'd be right. Fish and seafood features on the menu of some pretty classy restaurants in and around Nelson, from the Boatshed right there on the waterfront to the famous The Cut in town. But you don't have to pay top dollar to enjoy a bit of beautifully cooked blue cod while contemplating a million-dollar view.

In fact, your dinner will warm your knee as you nurse your newspaper-wrapped parcel of fish and chips on the drive to the Port Hills. There, on a fine evening — and not for nothing is Nelson known as the sunshine capital of New Zealand — you can watch the fishing boats come and go through the entrance to the Haven, and the historic lighthouse on the Boulder Bank wheeling its beam out across Tasman Bay.

Or you can head for the Domain and enjoy your meal at the exact geographic centre of New Zealand. When you're there, you'll know you're in the middle of something very special.

LATITUDE NELSON

Seafood, wine . . .
Nelson has it all.

101 MUST-DO'S
FOR KIWIS

Farewell Spit

You might be forgiven for thinking Farewell Spit is named for the last thing Abel Tasman did as he high-tailed it out of Murderers' Bay (which now bears the more marketing-savvy moniker, Golden Bay), after his unhappy brush with the tangata whenua. It was in fact named by James Cook, to mark the end of his first visit to New Zealand.

At the western end of Cook Strait, extending 35 kilometres east in a pleasant, sweeping arc east from Cape Farewell, which is the northernmost extremity of the South Island, the real Farewell Spit is the longest natural sandbar in the world.

Formed by the currents that sweep up the west coast of the South Island and curl around Cape Farewell into Cook Strait, the spit is composed entirely of bits of the ground-up mountains of the Main Divide.

Farewell Spit — the longest natural sandbar in the world.

In places, the sugary, white sand is piled 30 metres high (the Maori name, Te Onetahua, means 'heaped-up sand'). The spit was once largely covered in vegetation, but thanks to less-than-visionary farming techniques, the sand has for many years been given free rein. Selective planting and the encouragement of marram and spinifex grass are beginning to take effect, stabilising the peripatetic dunes.

Why bother? Well, the spit forms a kind of halfway hotel for migratory shore birds — no fewer than 83 species of wetland bird have been spotted here, including one of New Zealand's iconic long-distance travellers, the godwit — and it's also headquarters for breeding colonies of Australasian gannets. The significance of the habitat has been recognised in its status as a protected wetland.

Reached after a pretty drive from Collingwood, the spit is an experience that few other parts of New Zealand offer. Parts of it are like a little slice of Australia in Godzone, with the barren, blindingly reflective sands sandwiched between an azure sky and a cobalt sea. Other parts, behind the shelter of the dunes, are a wilderness of swamp. The view back across Golden Bay, with the elevated, snow-covered ranges of Kahurangi National Park beyond the coastal margins, is a bit of all right.

You can traverse the scorching sands of the northern margin of the spit by four-wheel-drive or quad bike. It's an exhilarating drive out to the Farewell Spit lighthouse, where a museum of sorts is maintained, documenting the lives and hardships of the keepers and their families. The lighthouse used to be at the very end, but as far as nature's concerned, the spit is a work in progress. It's still growing. Year by year, there's more of it to love.

The 102s

The natural spring at **Waikoropupu** near Farewell Spit. Simon Gilmore

Large colonies of Australian gannets call Farewell Spit home.

LATITUDE NELSON

Rameka Track

Mountain bikes are forbidden from the Abel Tasman National Park — all except for one section, the Rameka Track from Takaka Hill down into the Rameka Gorge. It's an old pack route from northwest Nelson's prospecting days and is still a registered road.

You'd be well-advised to involve two cars in your expedition — or one car with a dedicated driver. If you choose to use two vehicles, leave one in Takaka and take your bikes on the other along State Highway 60 back toward Motueka. You reach the track by taking the turnoff onto Canaan Road at the top of Takaka Hill — known locally as Marble Mountain, due to the dramatic outcrops of limestone and marble that occur here — and drive for 11 kilometres to the beginning of the track, the Harwood's Hole car park. (Harwood's Hole is a limestone sinkhole — the deepest 'straight drop' in the country — and well worth the side trip to have a peer in.) From the car park, there's a four-wheel-drive

Enjoy views of Golden Bay (opposite) and Kahurangi National Park from the top of the Marble Mountain.

LATITUDE NELSON

track that you ride to reach the beginning of the Rameka Track itself.

The first section of the track is a gnarly, snaking trail through beech forest, with plenty of branches, tree roots, fallen logs, boulders and potholes to keep you concentrating. You'll have to dismount from time to time to cross the stream, but most of it can be negotiated from the saddle.

Presently, you emerge onto the tops to a panoramic view of Golden Bay, and the misty peaks of Kahurangi National Park to the west. You'll also get a pretty good sight of the track ahead as it plunges down into the gorge.

Then there's nothing for it but to stand up on your pedals, brace yourself and let your shocks do the work as you rattle down the track. It's narrow in places, and there's the odd sharp bend thrown in to keep things exciting. In no time flat, as it seems, you're down. Eventually you'll emerge onto State Highway 60; it's a shortish ride from this point to Takaka itself, where you can enjoy a cold drink, a couple of hours after setting out.

LATITUDE NELSON

101 MUST-DO'S FOR KIWIS

Spa and Well-being Destination

Like Coromandel far to the north, the Nelson district drew alternative lifestylers in the 1960s and 1970s like bees to a honey pot. You'd have to suppose they were a slightly shrewder breed down this way, though: whereas the Coromandel receives around three metres of rain every year, Nelson receives under a third of that, as well as over 2500 hours of sunshine.

There's the climate. But perhaps there are other factors at work, too. Nelson is the geographical centre of New Zealand, and maybe there's something that draws hither souls that crave centring. The surrounding countryside is rich in minerals: perhaps it has something to do with the influence of all those crystals. Cook Strait is a major migratory path for whales, and Golden Bay abounds with dolphins: could there be a mystical link here somewhere with *Homo sapiens* on their own spiritual journey?

Who can say? Whatever it is, and while most of the actual card-carrying, muslin-wearing hippies have moved on, physically or philosophically speaking, there's still a decidedly alternative cast to Nelson's population. It's a hotbed of arts, crafts and creativity — all those things you need to nurture inner peace and beauty.

Over the years, many hippies have converted to the notion that materialism does have its redeeming features. They've taken to supplementing green tea and lentils with smoked salmon and chardonnay, and these days they play their whale-song and sitar CDs through the really excellent sound system of their BMWs for nostalgia's sake.

There's a booming local market for alternative therapies such as aromatherapy, reflexology, herbal treatments, iridology and reiki. And you won't have to go too far to find classes in spiritual healing, meditation, Eastern arts and every possible variation on Pilates and yoga.

Healthy living is strongly advocated in these parts: there's someone around every corner who will encourage you to give fasting, cleansing, slow food, healthy cooking and fresh organic produce a go.

The reconstructed hippies have also recognised that nurturing inner peace and beauty is all very well, but the old exterior can do with a bit of a buff now and then too.

Catering to this need is a new set of residents skilled in such once-obscure arts as Feldenkrais, shiatsu and hot stone massage therapy.

Many of the luxury accommodation options available in the Nelson area now offer all kinds of pampering packages — massage services, facials, beauty treatments and exclusive spa regimes.

It's an alternative lifestyle, all right.

Treat yourself to a bit of a pamper at the Lodge at Paratiho Farms, Nelson.

12

Marlborough

The Marlborough Sounds are a scenic wonderland, easily appreciated from the sea (many of its prettiest spots are accessible only by water or by air), or on foot along the famous Queen Charlotte Track. The centre of the district is pretty little Picton, and just down the line there's Blenheim, centre of the fabulous Marlborough wine region.

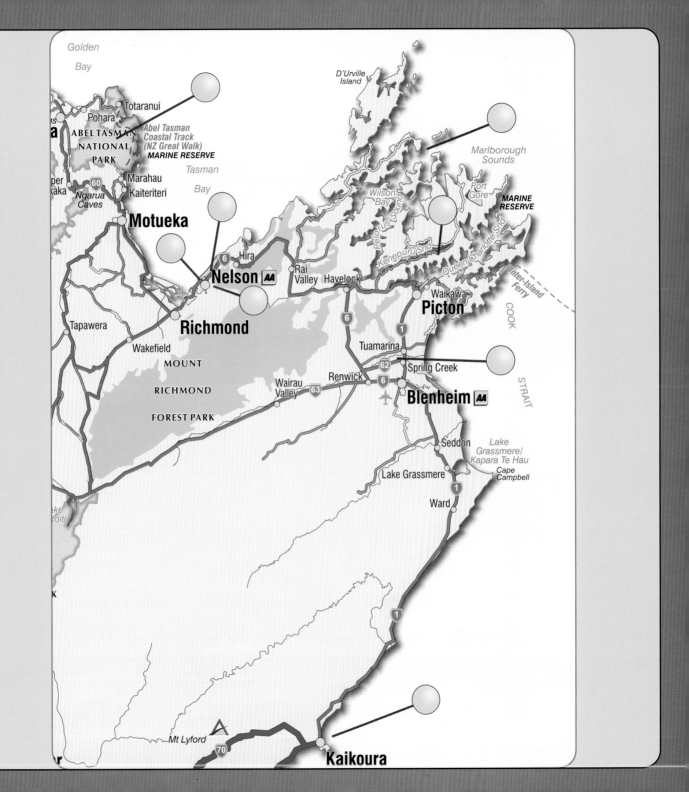

Marlborough Sounds

Marlborough must have been an amazing place to visit in the last Ice Age, when a fair chunk of the Southern Ocean was locked up in the Antarctic icebox. Marlborough was a region of high peaks divided by swooping plunges to river valleys — probably not unlike parts of Fiordland today. But then the earth warmed, the ice melted, the sea rose and it all went west.

On the bright side, however, the inundation of the great river valleys of

Find peace and tranquility in the Marlborough Sounds.

I LOVE YOU NEW ZEALAND

Love going to Blenheim and doing wine tasting, going to the chocolate shop and staying at Stonehaven Homestay. Shannon Hanson

I've only been to Marlborough Sounds once, but the days that my wife and I spent in an isolated bach accessible only by water were amongst the most perfect moments of our lives. The serenity and beauty of this place sum up the best that New Zealand has to offer to us. David Walker Bell

DESTINATION MARLBOROUGH

ancient Marlborough produced the internationally famous sounds. We had not so much lost a bunch of rivers as gained one of the prettiest waterways in the world.

You'd be forgiven for thinking James Cook had a bit of a thing for George III's wife, Queen Charlotte, because he named a number of bits of the world after her. The queen never knew what an honour Cook did her when he named one of the Marlborough Sounds after her. He knew a pretty waterway when he saw one, and Queen Charlotte Sound, with its mirror-calm channels, its maze of deep coves and secluded bays with songbird-haunted forest right down to the water's edge was doubtless one of the prettiest he visited, because it is still stunning today.

Ship Cove, where Cook careened his ship *Endeavour* in 1770, is accessible by road, like many of the prime spots in and around Queen Charlotte and neighbouring Kenepuru Sound. Fortunately there are alternatives in the form of water taxis or charter boats.

The hub of the sounds is Picton, which is the South Island terminal of the Interislander ferry service and point of departure for any number of sightseeing and nature-watching tours. Nearby, the little town of Havelock is the gateway to Kenepuru and Pelorus sounds. It is also the centre of the local aquaculture industry specialising in green-lipped mussels, which go down a treat with a glass of Marlborough sauvignon blanc.

DESTINATION MARLBOROUGH

Explore the sounds by kayak.

Marlborough Wine Trail

You don't have to go too far back— a matter of 30 years or so — to find yourself contemplating a bleak period in our history when wine was a sheila's drink. The ladies in question were confronted with a choice that boiled down to white (Blue Nun, Black Tower or Wohnsiedler) or red (Cold Duck with bubbles or imported chianti without bubbles!).

The Marlborough region must blush to recall that the first grapes to be planted on a commercial footing there in 1973 were Müller Thurgau, a varietal that doesn't need the process of drying to taste like raisins, and which produces a wine that savours on the palate like, well, a packet of raisins.

Since then, however, things have changed a bit. Quite a bit. With nearly 8,000 hectares in grapes, Marlborough is now New Zealand's largest wine-growing region. There are over 40 vineyards there, and a list of the names reads like the line-up of labels on the bottles gracing the honours table at international wine festivals. There's Allan Scott, Vavasour, Grove Mill, Mount Riley and, of course, Cloudy Bay, whose

Marlborough is world famous for its wines — and the food's damn good as well.

DESTINATION MARLBOROUGH

sauvignon blancs are of such consistent excellence that they have become the flagship of the formidable armada that sallies forth to titillate and tantalise the palates of the world.

Each Cloudy Bay sauvignon blanc is unmistakeably a child of its times and climes, vivid, dry and fragrant as the evening of a Marlborough summer's day. There's a pleasing complexity of flavours, with citrus and honey playing a kind of test match in the centre of your palate, a close-fought encounter where wine-making, ultimately, is the winner on the day.

For most, a visit to Cloudy Bay is the highlight of a star-studded wine tour. You can get about under your own steam (provided you keep an eye on your driver to make sure they're using the spittoon), or you can join an organised tour. Because there are so many cellar doors in a comparatively confined area, it's possible to cycle around many of them, and you can also hire a pony and trap to get about in real style.

Blenheim, the centre of the district, has a decent line-up of cafés and restaurants serving local specialities — such as mussels or blue cod from the Sounds, or lamb from down the line in Canterbury.

Like a Cloudy Bay sav blanc, the finish to a mellow summer's day is crisp in these parts, and the sight of the sunset over the mountains beyond the vineyards is the stuff that goosebumps are made of.

I LOVE YOU NEW ZEALAND

Everybody needs to experience Marlborough's wine trails, even the locals! Get out and enjoy what the rest of New Zealand can't stop talking about. Toni McDonald

DESTINATION MARLBOROUGH

The stony soils of Marlborough are ideal for viticulture.

The Queen Charlotte Track

The Queen Charlotte differs from others in the network of New Zealand's Great Walks, in that the accommodation is in a different class to other bush-bashing experiences. There are no huts, so you're obliged to spend the three or four nights you're on the walk camping. If you don't have a tent, you'll just have to make do with hotels, hostels and luxury lodges. Bummer.

The most popular direction in which to do the track is inbound — that is, from Ship Cove (reached by sightseeing launch or water taxi) at the entrance to Queen Charlotte Sound back to Anakiwa. The total distance is 71 kilometres, but since most of the track is accessible by water taxi, you can do as much or as little of it as you wish.

The Queen Charlotte Track is very well graded. The walking is comparatively easy, although the section from Punga Cove to Portage is dry, which not only means there's no one to sell you a beer, but you'll also have to weigh yourself down with bottled water.

The views of the sounds — both the picturesque, bush-fringed bays and inlets of Queen Charlotte Sound itself, and neighbouring Kenepuru Sound from the ridges — are magic. There's plenty of historical interest along the way. Ship Cove, where the track begins, was one of Captain James Cook's favourite anchorages: he visited no fewer than five times, and there is a monument to the great Yorkshireman in the reserve near the jetty. Resolution

The Queen Charlotte Track offers spectacular vistas of bush and the Marlborough Sounds.

In most parts the track is well graded.

DESTINATION MARLBOROUGH

Bay and Endeavour Inlet, which are among the first stops on your way along the track, are named for his ships.

Portage, at about the three-quarter mark, is so-named because it is the spot at which Maori travellers would bodily haul their waka up and over the ridge to save themselves days of paddling from Kenepuru Sound to Torea Bay in Queen Charlotte.

The best view to be had on the walk is from a vantage point you reach on a short side trip from the main track after the steep climb from Portage. It gives a spectacular view of Queen Charlotte, Kenepuru and Mahau Sounds and — always gratifying, this — the long ridge you've traversed from Punga Cove.

The Queen Charlotte Track is a solid four days' walk, but you can do it in style. Few tracks, even in New Zealand, offer the opportunity to finish a day's tramping with a sundowner, a soak in a spa bath and a dreamless sleep in crisp linen.

It's roughing it, Jim, but not as we know it.

I LOVE YOU NEW ZEALAND

One of our best winter escapes was staying at a nearby bay and walking to Ship's Cove and back. A fabulous place to visit and we reeled in the fish too. Dawn Falkner

DESTINATION MARLBOROUGH

The track is also suitable for mountain bikers.

West Coast

The West Coast is iconic Kiwi country. The landscapes are as unusual as they are spectacular: the odd-looking Pancake Rocks, the dazzling glaciers, the serene lakes such as Lake Matheson, the limestone country of the Paparoa National Park and the rugged grandeur of the Buller Gorge. The people are hard as nails — you'd have to be to dream up something like the Hokitika Wild Foods Festival — but have hearts of gold.

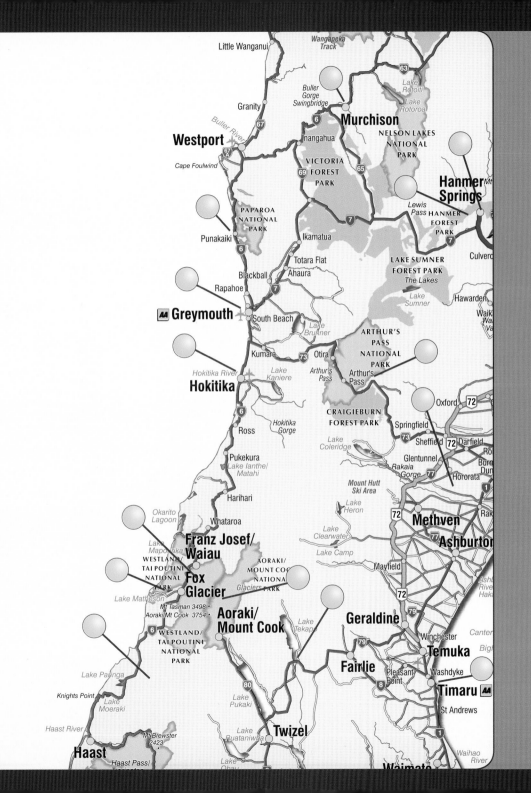

Buller Gorge

If you're driving from Nelson to Westport, you'll first pick up the Buller just past Glenhope, about 30 kilometres as the kereru flies from where the mighty river arises from Lake Rotoiti. The point on the road is called Kawatiri, which is thought to mean 'deep and swift'. There's no prizes for guessing why the Maori gave this name to the river that the European settlers subsequently named after pioneer Charles Buller.

The Buller will be your guide for the next 150-odd kilometres of some of the most scenic driving anywhere. It draws you into its steep, bush-clad gorge then heads for the coast.

It's always been a mixed blessing being a passenger through here. On the one hand, you get to admire the scenery — the sheer walls of the gorge rising mist-veiled from the river on its stony course. On the other, your fate is in your driver's hands, and you spend much of your time fervently hoping their eyes are glued to the road.

Spare a thought, then, as you negotiate the various hair-raising bends in the road, for those who travelled with the Newman brothers who ran a coach service through the gorge at the beginning of the last century. And when you're done shuddering at the prospect of riding in a rattling, lurching, swaying four-in-hand through the gorge before the road was sealed, think about the Newman boys' next venture — flogging the Cadillac service cars that replaced their horses along the same tortuous stretch.

After a brief respite on the gravel flat where the little settlement of Inangahua Junction sits, you're back in the gorge, the Lower Buller Gorge, this time. You might have thought the road was hairy back up

the way — there's certainly no shortage of sharp bends in the narrow road — but the Lower Buller features the sharpest bends of the lot. At Hawke's Crag, where the roadway has literally been carved out of a stony bluff, the remnant of the crag still overhangs the tight, blind corner, allowing very little headway for tall vehicles. There's also a thrilling drop to the river on your right.

In spite of it all, though, by the time you've issued forth with the river onto Addison's Flat, the broad, swampy hinterland of Westport, it all seems too soon. When you reach the turn-off (north onto State Highway 67 to Westport and, beyond it, Karamea, or south on State Highway 6 to Greymouth and South Westland), you'll just about be ready to turn around and do the gorge again.

I LOVE YOU NEW ZEALAND

The swing bridge and flying fox on State Highway 6 on the route to Westport is a MUST! Denise Coyle

PHOTO NEW ZEALAND/STEVE BICKNELL

The Buller Gorge wends its way to the West Coast.

Fox & Franz Josef Glaciers

FOX GLACIER GUIDING

Many of the crinklier bits of New Zealand's geography were formed by the slow but insistent action of glaciers. We were at the peak of our glaciation a few million years ago, during the last Ice Age, long before they invented *Homo sapiens*, let alone tourism or digital photography.

Although the earth has warmed up a bit and most of our glaciers have melted, happily there's still a few lying around available to be inspected and have their picture taken.

The unique feature of the Fox and Franz Josef glaciers is their accessibility. Franz Josef Glacier, for example — named for the Austrian Emperor Franz Josef I by his loyal subject, the surveyor Julius von Haast, in 1865 — is but a short walk from the car park off State Highway 6 in South Westland, and an equally short drive from top-class accommodation.

The approach is pretty enough in its own right, winding through typical West Coast rain forest. And the sight at the end of it — the jumbled icefall of the glacier's snout above its placid terminal lake — isn't something you see every day. If you hang around long enough, increasingly in the era of climate change, you may be favoured with the sight of an iceberg calving from the glacier's snout, crashing into the lake below. Bear this in mind if you decide to go kayaking on the lake: when the guides tell you not to approach the terminal face, there's a ten-tonne reason for it.

You can discover Fox Glacier on a half-day walk.

101 MUST-DO'S FOR KIWIS

You can join a guided tour up onto the glacier itself, and the more intrepid can explore the luminous ice caves and crevasses on its flanks. A more demanding climb alongside the glacier will take you up to the névé (the snow reservoir that supplies the icefall) high up in the Southern Alps. Then again, you can accomplish the same ascent by helicopter, getting a once-in-a-lifetime view along the way.

The more southerly of the West Coast's famous glaciers, the Fox, was named for noted nineteenth-century surveyor and politician, Sir William Fox. It requires a little more effort to visit on foot than Franz Josef, but is just as readily accessible by air. Whether you point and coo from your car as you drive by, take the time to tramp up the terminal face, fly over them or land on them, both glaciers can easily be incorporated into your unforgettable tour of the South Island.

I LOVE YOU NEW ZEALAND

Just another one of New Zealand's breathtaking places to visit. Took our children there in the 1960s and then our grandchildren in the 1990s. Still the same awe-inspiring scenery.
Robin Spillane

See the ice formations for yourself.

FOX GLACIER GUIDING

Lake Matheson

If you find yourself in a reflective mood on the West Coast, you'll also find you're in good company. Dotted in the ancient shingle fans laid down by the advance and more recent retreat of the glaciers, you'll find a number of jewel-like lakes holding a mirror to the sky and the Southern Alps.

Most of the waterways in this part of the world reflect some pretty spectacular scenery when the conditions are right. After all, there's a bunch of alps looming over the lot of them, from the largest — Lake Brunner, close to the western approach to Arthur's Pass — to the smallest, among which is Lake Lyttle. Lakes Ianthe, Mahinapua and Mapourika all give a good account of themselves and the adjacent scenery, but the most spectacular and reliable of the lot is little Lake Matheson, reached by taking a short detour from State Highway 6 out towards Gillespie's Beach.

Matheson occupies a hollow in what was once the moraine of the Fox Glacier, dating from the chilly days 14,000 years ago when the icefall was rampant.

Like the other lakes on the West Coast, the waters are dark and tea-coloured, which is no coincidence, considering it's the tannin leached from the leaf litter on the floor of the age-old rainforests of Westland that give them this colour.

There's a walking track around the lake, and once you reach the western end, there's a platform from which to admire the main attraction: Aoraki/Mount Cook, reflected upside down in the depths.

The wall of rainforest around Matheson protects it from anything other than serious breezes, so the surface is usually mirror-calm. It's possible to take a picture of Mount Cook

and its image and be quite unable to see which way up you should be holding the frame.

Lake Matheson is in the Westland Tai Poutini National Park. The bush here is mature rimu and kahikatea, both of which like their roots wet. Their drooping foliage is the perfect frame for the view. Apart from birdsong, the only sound to break the hush is the slap-slap sound of sandflies being dispatched to the Other Side. Well-equipped visitors won't even be troubled by these little biters provided they've packed their insect repellant.

Several of the West Coast lakes have more than just a pretty face. If you ever get tired of just staring at the view you can paddle and fish on lakes Brunner and Mahinapua. And quite frankly, I wouldn't hold my breath on that score.

Lake Matheson is famous for its reflection of Mount Cook and Mount Tasman.

PHOTO NEW ZEALAND/STAN DANIELS

Punakaiki

Funny the Maori should have had a word that sounded so much like the English word for 'pancakes'. Funnier yet that it should have been applied to a place where the rock formations so closely resemble enormous, petrified stacks of pancakes.

The Maori name for the rocks, however, had nothing to do with pancakes. Puna means spring and kaiki is a misspelling of kaike, which means to lie heaped one above another. Punakaiki therefore means the spring where the rocks lie heaped up.

The business end of Dolomite Point in Westland cops some serious sea, and over the centuries, the 30-million-year-old limestone of which it is composed has eroded. Limestone is a sedimentary rock — it's composed of the remains of shellfish that lived and died in the primeval sea, their shells laid down in layer upon layer and gradually compressed and petrified into rock.

Some years were evidently good years for shellfish. Others were decidedly dodgy, and the layer of rock corresponding to the off years is less dense and therefore softer. When the sea gets its claws into the layered limestone, it quickly strips the softer layers away, leaving the harder layers behind. That's what gives the Pancake Rocks their distinctive stacked appearance.

You reach this geological marvel after a short walk through a pocket of dense bush. Access out onto the rock formation itself is by a short gravel track and a series of boardwalks.

The same erosion that has left some layers intact and carried others away has also sculpted Dolomite Point into a series of caves and surge channels. On a calm day, you can hear and feel the water heaving and breathing under your feet, and you can watch the incoming and outgoing swells gently combing the kelp in the blowholes. On a rough day, the sea thunders into the

sea caves, and forces its way up through vertical shafts in great plumes of white foam. It's an awe-inspiring display of the sheer weight and energy of waves.

The same limestone of which the Pancake Rocks are formed persists inland from Punakaiki in the Paparoa National Park. The park is endowed with some fascinating landforms: caves, sinkholes, and great white-walled gorges through which pure, limestone-filtered streams and rivers flow. Paparoa, for this reason, is a playground for cavers, rafters, kayakers and trampers alike.

The coastline north from Punakaiki to Karamea, the northernmost extent of the road, is quite beautiful, with white-sand beaches and rugged headlands quarrelling with the Tasman Sea.

Flapjack Rocks just wouldn't have had the same ring, really. And as for Crêpe Rocks — they're definitely not that.

I LOVE YOU NEW ZEALAND

It's wild and wonderful scenery — get off the main tourist track at Punakaiki and explore to find more scenic treasures.
Naomi Hannah Brown

PHOTO NEW ZEALAND/ROB DRIESSEN

Millions of years of erosion have produced the Pancake Rocks.

South Westland

You won't be bothered by sandflies on Mount Everest, or in the Grand Canyon, or even on the Great Barrier Reef. So if you want the sandfly experience in a UNESCO World Heritage area, then you'll just have to go to South Westland.

The canny folk at UNESCO don't hand out World Heritage status to just any old bit of landscape. You've got to show them that your candidate piece of real estate possesses natural or cultural features that are of international significance.

They didn't need much persuasion with regard to the bottom left-hand corner of our little country, which takes in some of the other must-do areas canvassed in more detail in this book — Aoraki/Mount Cook, Fiordland and Mount Aspiring national parks, the glaciers, Lake Matheson and Haast's Blue Pools. But even if you've ticked these off your list, don't think for a moment you've exhausted the pleasures that South Westland has to offer.

Take the detour to Jackson Bay, the southernmost extent of the road on the West Coast of the South Island. It's a great little spot, full of history — various communities have had a crack at setting up here, with greater and lesser degrees of success. There was even a short-lived attempt to set up a planned community of Italian grapegrowers in the swampy hinterland of Jackson Bay, which probably didn't seem like a good idea even at the time. A landscape and locale more unlike the Mediterranean is hard to imagine.

There's a short walk from where a green house sports a sign reading 'End of the Road' through the bush to Smoothwater Bay, where you can fossick for greenstone and perhaps even spot a yellow-eyed penguin.

The fishing down here is pretty good too, and there are charters available to get you in amongst it. There's hunting and trout-fishing opportunities everywhere, and more tramping than you can poke a Leki pole at. Just don't forget your insect repellent.

Take a detour to Jackson Bay.

PHOTO NEW ZEALAND/STEVE BICKNELL

Alpine-Pacific Triangle, Canterbury & Mackenzie Country

It's often said about New Zealand that you can see something approximating any one of its scenic wonders elsewhere in the world, but nowhere else will you see them packed together as they are here. This region bears that observation out. From the gallic charm of Akaroa, the teeming marine life of Kaikoura, the mellow vineyards of Waipara and the farmland of the Canterbury Plains, up into the mountains, where Hanmer's hot springs seethe and Aoraki/Mount Cook presides over a parliament of mountains, reflected in the high country lakes . . . Stop, stop! You're drooling.

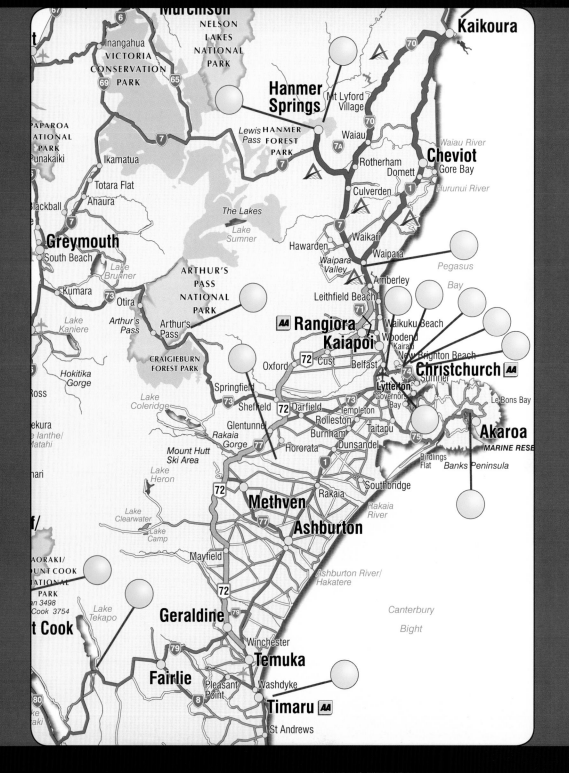

Akaroa

In an hour's easy drive from Christchurch and just over the crest of the hill you see Akaroa Harbour — literally 'long harbour' in Maori — opening dramatically before you, the land dropping steeply to turquoise sea.

Akaroa is a tangible link to one of the tantalising 'what-ifs' of New Zealand history: the attempt mounted by the Nanto-Bordelaise Immigration Company to annex the South Island for France in 1840. A boat load of Frenchmen arrived in August, to find the English had beaten them to annexing New Zealand by three months. *Zut alors*! But all was not lost: the French were permitted to stay, and Akaroa became a little slice of Bordeaux in the deep south. It has retained the Gallic flavour: some of the street names — Rue Jolie, Rue Balguerie — and many of the names of shops and businesses are, 'ow you say, a giveaway.

As if to bless those French settlers' choice of the site for their colonial enterprise, the land round about the harbour yields every kind of produce you need to live with true Gallic panache — olives and olive oil, walnuts, cheese

Akaroa township retains its French flavour.

PHOTO NEW ZEALAND/ROB DRIESSEN

PHOTO NEW ZEALAND/ROB DRIESSEN

Tiny Hector's dolphins are regular visitors to Akaroa Harbour.

from the famous Barry's Bay fromagerie, and wine from the several vineyards that are coaxing surprising results from Banks Peninsula's volcanic soil. The harbour itself hosts an aquaculture venture raising superb salmon, and the rugged coastline is a prime blue cod fishery. You can enjoy the fruits of land and sea at any one of a dozen excellent cafés and restaurants.

Those who wish to stay on in Akaroa can choose from backpacker to luxury bed-and-breakfast accommodation.

The area's unique history is celebrated by the Akaroa Museum and the Akaroa Historic Walk, and the local community is sprinkled with artists and craftspeople, whose wares are on display or for purchase in the many little galleries and shops. One shop on the wharf sells the intriguing locally grown and widely prized paua pearl.

Another major attraction of the area is the chance to take a cruise to observe the local wildlife, including penguins, seals and the area's resident population of Hector's dolphins. These are not only the smallest, but also the rarest dolphins in the world: there's only 17,000 of them, all in New Zealand waters.

Akaroa is also the starting and finishing point of the Banks Peninsula Walkway, the perfect way to see this rugged and beautiful part of the country.

Aoraki/Mount Cook: Sky-Piercer

The Southern Alps are an impressive sight in their own right, but 3754 metre Mount Cook is something else. The Maori who shivered on the trail of pounamu — greenstone — in the deep south named the great peak Aoraki, or sky-piercer, and that's precisely what it does.

Since the early days of European settlement, the Mount Cook area has attracted a steady stream of sightseers and adventurers alike. In the early days, it was a rugged trip by horse and coach to get to the isolated and aptly named Hermitage Hotel; a motor service was established in 1906, but the Hermitage was a marginal venture for several years even after the government took it over in 1909. Today, however, with good roads, helicopter and fixed-wing air access, there's a thriving settlement at Mount Cook village.

There are levels of accommodation to suit all budgets, from the bare-basics Whitehorse Hill campground run by the Department of Conservation to the opulence of the Hermitage itself. Whatever extras your money can buy, though, a million-dollar view of Australasia's highest peak comes as standard.

Naturally enough, the area is a paradise for alpine pursuits. The faint of heart can

Take a stroll in Hooker Valley — Mount Cook lives up to its name as a sky-piercer.

MACKENZIE TOURISM

just look, whether from the windows of their car or from a café, where New Zealand's mischievous mountain parrot, the kea, will often keep you company. Looking is, after all, the second-best way to experience the vertiginous swoop of rocky buttresses and sheer icefalls, the smooth perfection of elevated snowfields, and the jumble of the vast glaciers.

The best way, of course, is to get up there amongst it all. You can do that by taking a scenic flight by helicopter or plane, and you can even land at various points in the UNESCO World Heritage-listed Aoraki/ Mount Cook National Park, including on the mighty Tasman Glacier. The Tasman offers one of the world's greatest heli-skiing runs.

There is plenty of scope here too for trampers, climbers and mountaineers of all abilities. There are brisk day-walks, such as the stroll through tussock land

Explore the Hooker Glacier by boat.

and shattered moraine to the terminal face of the Hooker Glacier. For the more experienced and intrepid, there are solid tramps to the Ball Pass and Mueller huts. And for the mountaineer there are several demanding peaks and alpine passes, such as the Copland Pass, which crosses from the Hooker Valley to the West Coast, and there is the ultimate challenge: a summit assault on old Sky-Piercer himself.

The Southern Alps are spectacular from the air.

101 MUST-DO'S FOR KIWIS

Arthur's Pass National Park

No one really remembers who Arthur was (he was surveyor Arthur Dudley Dobson, who pioneered the route that bears his name in 1864), but this is his pass. It is the lowest of the three alpine passes that give road access from the east coast of the South Island to Westland — most of the time, as half the fun of driving over in winter is checking the road status reports to see whether you can get across the pass. The highest point in the road is 920 metres above sea level, so anything resembling a decent dump of snow and you can bet you'll be changing your plans.

Travel on the TranzAlpine to Arthur's Pass station.

TRANZSCENIC

If, on the other hand, you'd rather take the uncertainty out of it all, then the thing to do is catch the train. After all, not only is the TranzAlpine Railway one of the prettiest rail journeys in the world, it's also one of the very few passenger rail experiences we Kiwis have left.

It doesn't matter which direction you travel, the TranzAlpine gives its passengers a front-row seat in a kind of scenic slideshow. From the Canterbury Plains, the route ascends through tussock and beech forest to the pass itself. Along the way, the alps are sliced up by river valleys, complete with great rivers, including the mighty braided Waimakariri.

There's a little settlement at Arthur's Pass itself, and there's plenty to do there. In the winter, there's a couple of skifields within a few minutes' drive. Year round, in the Arthur's Pass National Park area there's some of the best walking, tramping and mountaineering to be had anywhere. There are more than 30 back-country huts linked by a network of tracks to suit all abilities and ambitions, and several significant peaks within comfortable range.

Once over the pass, road and rail descend steeply through the Otira River gorge — literally, in the case of the railway, which plunges through the spectacular feat of engineering that is the Otira rail tunnel. The landscape changes dramatically, with the alpine flora giving way to West Coast rainforest. Road and rail together follow the course of the Taramakau River to Kumara Junction, from whence it's north to Greymouth and the Buller district or South to Hokitika, South Westland and Haast.

I LOVE YOU NEW ZEALAND

One of my favorite parts of New Zealand. I regularly cross through this region en route to the west coast. Walk the Punchbowl Falls and be amazed by the sheer power of the water and the stunning mountain backdrops. Chris Cameron

PHOTO NEW ZEALAND/GEOFF MASON

The mighty Waimakariri River.

101 MUST-DO'S FOR KIWIS

Canterbury Plains

Hot-Air Ballooning

BALLOON ADVENTURES UP UP AND AWAY LIMITED © 2005

A still morning is what you want: after all, set yourself aloft at the mercy of the winds when the famous Canterbury nor'wester is due and it's next stop Patagonia.

On a frosty morning, you're generally glad of the burner when the big LPG jets are lit up. All hands hold the neck of the balloon away from the flames as they're directed into its belly. Slowly, almost imperceptibly, with a ball-gown rustle, it inflates and heaves itself off the ground. At a certain point, the basket rocks upright, and then the focus shifts to keeping it in position until the passengers are aboard.

Once everyone's clambered into the basket — for reasons that are likely to have more to do with style than sheer practicality, wickerwork is still traditional — your captain gives her a few more blasts on the burner and gently, so gently you hardly notice, you're airborne and rising.

It's probably the most relaxing form of transport ever devised, like floating down a river on an inner-tube, only in mid-air. Surprising as it may seem, you can even assert some kind of control over the direction of your drift. Because air moves about in layers, it's a matter of moving up or down until you find yourself in a favourable airstream.

If this is your first time on a hot-air balloon, you may find yourself gripping the sides of the basket a little more tightly than is strictly necessary. After all, it's kind of hard to believe that you're being kept a hundred metres aloft by nothing more than a big hamper, some rope and a few hundred square metres of the stuff they make boxer shorts out of.

But in the end there's nothing to do but relax and admire the view — the Canterbury Plains laid like a tablecloth to the very foot of the Southern Alps in the west, their expanse a patchwork of crop and pasture.

You can help your pilot keep a lookout

BALLOON ADVENTURES UP UP AND AWAY LIMITED © 2005

I LOVE YOU NEW ZEALAND

Magic!! Definitely worth getting out of bed early for — a day to remember forever. Very lucky to have had the chance to do this — give it a go even if you live there.
Lynette Crooks

Breathtaking views from above! Made us appreciate the uniqueness of Canterbury: Southern Alps to the west, flat patchwork-quilt effect of the plains below and the Pacific Ocean to the east — we really do have it all! Joanne Small

for power lines and horses. Horses can't look up, so if the balloon's shadow falls across them or they're startled by a staccato blast on the burner, they start doing rapid circuits of their paddocks, which is funny for everyone but the horse.

Landings can be a bit hairy, depending on the skill of your pilot and the strength and consistency of the breeze. But once on the ground, you can round it all off with breakfast, a glass of bubbly and memories of a once-in-a-lifetime experience.

Go hot-air ballooning for a once-in-a-lifetime experience.

179

Christchurch City

CHRISTCHURCH & CANTERBURY TOURISM

Trams still ply the streets of central Christchurch.

Christchurch is living proof that you could take the colonists out of England, but you couldn't take England out of the colonists. The whole project was designed to create a little slice of Kent in the antipodes, and by crikey, they came close to realising that ambition.

They were assisted by the geographical features of the site. Deep, gravelly soils laid down by the erosion of the Southern Alps met and mixed with the mineral riches liberally sprinkled about the district by the volcanic activity that gave us Banks Peninsula, with the consequence that things grow pretty well here. And since summers are real summers and winters are real winters in Christchurch, the English flora that the settlers brought with them to plant here adapted painlessly to their new southern habitat. They do a nice rolling lawn in Christchurch. And you don't have to travel halfway round the world to see an English autumn: just visit Hagley Park when the poplars, birches and oaks are dressed in their autumnal golds and reds. Nor do the displays of daffodil, jonquil, camellia and rose along the banks of the Avon leave much to be desired of an Old English spring.

Happily, the bewhiskered gents who roughed out Christchurch on a scrap of paper over a snifter or two of brandy at their club left lots of space for the floral bounty of the Old Country to flourish.

I LOVE YOU NEW ZEALAND

There is an inexpensive walking tour of the city that leaves from a booth in Cathedral Square which is a really good introduction to the central city and some of the history of the buildings. A worthwhile start to any holiday there! The market in the square and of course the cathedral itself are also worth a look.

Andrea Lavarre-Waters

The 165 hectare Hagley Park, directly adjacent to the civic centre, is a jewel, its network of pleasant tracks heavily patronised by joggers and cyclists. The park's kaleidoscopic display, together with the bounty of lovingly maintained private gardens, have seen Christchurch described not only as New Zealand's 'Garden City', but 'Garden City of the World' in the 1997 Nations in Bloom International Competition.

That's the backdrop. The city, of course, also boasts a little facsimile of an English cathedral. Built over the course of 37 years from locally quarried stone, Christchurch Cathedral was opened in 1901. And the Avon River, which meanders between manicured banks right through the heart of the city, and the place and street names — Gloucester Street, Worcester Street, Oxford Square, Cambridge Terrace — are all perfectly in keeping with the whole Anglo thing.

And to cap it all off, because the prevailing wind over the Canterbury Plains is a dry nor'wester, cars don't rust here. Christchurch sports the highest population of English cars in everyday use in the country. Little wonder English visitors dodging Hillman Minxes and Ford Anglias in the shadow of the cathedral think they've strayed into some kind of eccentric theme park, or fallen into a time warp that's placed them right back in Blighty, 30 years ago.

Coastal Kaikoura

There was a time, not so long ago in the grand scale of things, when the whale-watching industry in New Zealand did most of its observation of whales over the sights of cannons firing explosive harpoons. And one of the centres of this gory trade was Kaikoura, where a convergence of warm oceanic currents and the proximity of the edge of the continental shelf create freakishly fertile oceanic conditions. The local profusion of the type of greebly that skulks at the bottom of the food chain makes this bit of coast a kind of smorgasbord for marine life, including the largest marine creatures of all, the great whales.

Dozens of whale species are represented in these waters: from the little Hector's dolphin — the smallest cetacean in the world and one of the rarest — to humpback and right whales. These whales, whose migratory patterns once put them within easy reach of Kaikoura's shore-whaling station but now bring them about as close to whale-watching tourists as they can get without actually hitting the beach.

The whale- and dolphin-watching industry in Kaikoura is a flagship of the

Watch out for the albatrosses.

ENCOUNTER KAIKOURA/DENNIS BURMAN

ENCOUNTER KAIKOURA/DENNIS BURMAN

I LOVE YOU NEW ZEALAND

My 91-year-old father and I went out on the whale-watch trip. We saw dolphins, albatrosses, mollymawks and whales and at the end of the day my father rated it as one of the best days of his life. As a child my parents took me to Goose Bay every holiday and we used to see huge pods of dolphins and many whales from a distance. Nothing could beat this trip though. Herewina Banks

Hector's dolphins putting on a display.

shift from the kind of 'extraction' activity that once drove our economy — mining, forestry, whaling — to 'attraction' activities, where the tourism dollar is key.

And tourists flock here. They mill around the booking offices in the pleasant little town of Kaikoura about as excitedly as a pod of dolphins among a school of pilchards. For very few places in the world can offer encounters with the giants of the deep as intimate and awe-inspiring as those available here.

You can watch them from the air, on whale- and dolphin-spotting scenic flights by helicopter or fixed-wing aircraft. You can watch them from the shore, as they cruise in the deep water only a hundred metres off the rocky beach. You can watch them from spitting distance from a chartered launch. Depending on weather and sea conditions and the mood of the relevant marine mammal species, you can even swim with dolphins, whales and seals here — the ultimate experience, unless you count Jonah's.

And speaking of eating, Kaikoura town and district feature a profusion of top-class cafés and restaurants where — as you would expect in an area named for an ancient Maori navigator's seafood mixed grill — the pièce de résistance is the bounty of the sea.

Let's face it, there's something fishy about the whole place — in the nicest possible way.

Hanmer Springs

ALPINE PACIFIC TOURISM/THRILLSEEKERS

Winter time at Hanmer Springs can be beautiful.

There's only one thing better than lounging in soft mineral water heated by thermal springs, and that's lying in soft mineral water heated by thermal springs when the ground around you is covered with snow and there's a biting southerly blowing down from the tops.

Outside Iceland, there are few places in the world where you can enjoy this experience. In less culturally sensitive times, you could excavate a little pool in the Ketetahi Stream high on the slopes of the North Island's Mount Tongariro in winter, but that opportunity no longer exists.

That leaves Hanmer Springs, which has the additional and winning advantage of being fully accessible to all.

The thermal springs at Hanmer were discovered by William Jones in 1859, who noticed steam drifting across his path when he was poking about on the banks of the Percival River in the Amuri district. The springs were subsequently developed as a health spa, at a time when belief in the therapeutic qualities of geothermal springs was at its height. A large, Art Deco-style hotel was constructed nearby in the 1930s, and a small township grew up around it, named after Sir Thomas Hanmer, whose fame today is obscure but who was an Englishman with an undoubtedly steamy disposition.

Today, Hanmer is a thriving town, not unlike a scaled-down Queenstown.

The thermal resort has been extensively re-developed, and the spring's water diverted into a number of pools with a range of temperatures so that you can ease yourself into the really hot stuff by degrees. There are dozens of accommodation options, ranging from a well-appointed campground to the refurbished Heritage Hanmer Springs Hotel. While the thermal pools are the focal point of the district, there's plenty else to do. Hanmer has a good range of shops, cafés, art galleries and restaurants. The wider district, particularly the Waiau River valley, has plenty to offer the adventurous, from rafting, jet boating and kayaking to horse riding, bungy jumping, quad biking and off-roading in eight-wheel Argo all-terrain vehicles. There's also plenty of skiing and snowboarding terrain, from the small Amuri field to the heli-skiing possibilities of Mount Lyford and the surrounding ranges.

Hanmer is the inland apex of the Alpine-Pacific Triangle touring route, and can be incorporated into a circular tour that also takes in Kaikoura and the vineyards of Waipara. What's more, it's only a short detour from State Highway 7, which crosses the Lewis Pass to the West Coast and features another well-developed thermal resort, Maruia Springs, en route.

There are plenty of ways of getting into hot water in this little country of ours, but you won't beat this one.

Splashing around at Hanmer Springs Thermal Pools & Spa.

Get into hot water in Hanmer Springs.

Lake Tekapo

The great high tussock plains beyond the first range of mountains bordering the Canterbury region are collectively known as the Mackenzie Country, after a stockman who drove 1000 head of sheep this way in 1855. Trouble was, they weren't James McKenzie's sheep, and nor did they belong to the man who engaged his droving services. He was convicted and jailed for being 'in the company of' 1000 sheep that didn't belong to him.

McKenzie is commemorated not only in the name of the region (and even though the spelling differs from his), but also in the various legends that subsequently sprang up surrounding his rustling prowess and the supposedly supernatural powers of his sharp-eyed dog, Friday.

McKenzie, Friday and the other pioneers of the district are commemorated by the Church of the Good Shepherd and the fine statue of a border collie on the shores of Lake Tekapo. In lieu of a stained glass window, the little stone church has a clear pane overlooking Tekapo and the Mackenzie Basin — ornament enough indeed. The church was opened in 1935, and has proved a focal point for visitors to this area ever since.

The unsurpassed clarity of the air up here made it a natural choice for the location of the internationally renowned

Lake Pukaki's cloudy blue waters are the result of rock flour in suspension.

MACKENZIE TOURISM

Mount John Observatory. There's a fair few stars in the night sky, and it seems a lot of them are on full display of a clear Mackenzie Country night. Educational tours of the observatory are available to the public, and staff run nightly star-gazing sessions, where visitors can use telescopes, binoculars and the naked eye to find their way about the heavens.

By day, the view's still pretty spectacular. The arid splendour of the Mackenzie Country is laid out before you, limited to the west by the Main Divide and dominated, as are all central South Island vistas, by Aoraki/Mount Cook.

The ice-fed waters of Lake Tekapo and of nearby Lake Pukaki are cold and coloured intense blue. The colossal, heavy tread of glaciation grinds stone to fine dust and it is this 'rock flour', suspended in the water, that gives rise to their brilliant turquoise tint. The surrounding russet, gold and umbers of the tussock is studded in season by the lupins that have colonised the southern high country.

A colourful scene indeed.

I LOVE YOU NEW ZEALAND

It's a magical, peaceful and tranquil and a truly great place to holiday. Nothing beats skimming stones on the shore of Lake Tekapo.
Karen Bamford

MACKENZIE TOURISM

The sheepdog statue at the Church of the Good Shepherd pays tribute to working dogs.

Wanaka

The entire Southern Lakes region of the central South Island is a playground. Wanaka is a popular holiday spot for mainlanders and overseas visitors alike. The lake and the mighty Clutha River that empties it, plus the surrounding mountains and rivers, and especially the wonderland that is Mount Aspiring National Park, offer unsurpassed recreational opportunities.

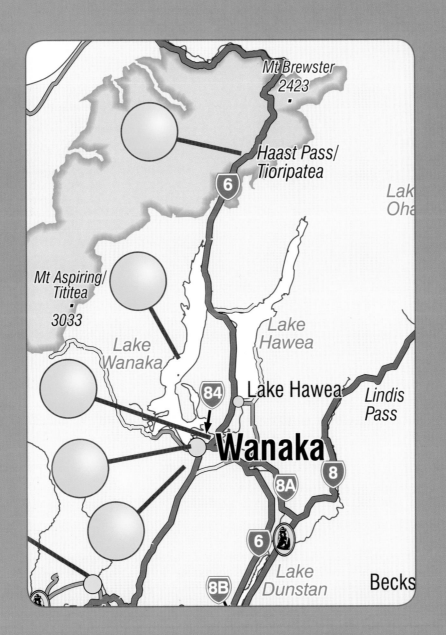

Cross-country Skiing

Take to the snow
at SnowFarm.

LAKE WANAKA TOURISM

It was one of the tragedies of history that skiing was invented at a time when the technology of ski lifts lay nearly 4000 years in the future. And given that the inhabitants of ancient Scandinavia depended on skis to supply their land transport requirements, you'd expect the major centres of Nordic population to have occurred exclusively at the foot of hills.

That's because we tend to identify skiing with its downhill variant where, as the name suggests, you start at the top of a hill and slide down to the bottom. Nordic skiing, by contrast, can be done in the absence of gradients and even actually uphill.

How, you ask, is this possible?

Well, in the remote past, seal skins were fitted to the bottom of the skis. When you moved the ski forward, the sleek fur slid over the snow, creating only a little added friction. Try moving it backwards, however, against the grain, and the fur resisted. This meant you could slide one ski forward, then the other, without slipping backwards between 'steps'. The bindings on Nordic skis, what's more, are anchored only at the toe to facilitate this 'stepping' motion. It's possible to cover great distances on Nordic skis expending little more effort than you'd use walking. This is why Nordic skiing is commonly referred to as 'cross-country' skiing.

These days, of course, we have a sophisticated array of synthetic materials available to us, and instead of seal skins, cross-country skiers use lengths of that stuff they make lint-removing gloves from — a sort of velvety fabric that has thousands of miniature pouches in it that lie flat if rubbed one way and puff up and snag that pesky cat fur when rubbed the other. Ever wondered how Scandinavians keep their suits so free of lint? Well, now you know.

The other main difference to downhill skiing is, of course, the act of turning, given the toe-only fastening of the skis to your boots. Nordic skiers turn their skis by performing an odd-looking kneeling manoeuvre called 'telemarking'. It can take a bit of getting used to, but once mastered, telemarking feels sort of liberated by comparison.

New Zealand's only dedicated cross-country ski facility is located on the Pisa Range above Lake Wanaka, where over 50 kilometres of tracks give peerless views of the Southern Alps.

Imagine eyeballing Mount Aspiring and, farther off, Aoraki/Mount Cook from your perch, muscles pleasantly tired, with only a swish-swish sound to disturb the solitude as you remove the lint from your trousers. Magic.

Young or old — there's skiing for everyone at Cardrona Alpine Resort.

LAKE WANAKA TOURISM

Kicking the Autumn Leaves

Wellington poet Amelia Nurse has written about 'the lake effect' — the noticeable calming and smoothing of the ripples in brow and soul that occurs when you find yourself on the shores of a lake with time to spare.

There's probably no better place to experience the lake effect than at Lake Wanaka. There's a variety of ways you can interact with the lake — it's an aquatic playground for anglers, water-skiers, jet-skiers, jet-boaters, sailors, fizz-boaters, swimmers and windsurfers . . . and more.

But there's also a network of walkways around the lake, giving glimpses, opening vistas over the water, and generally exposing you to maximum lake effect.

There are some really staunch walks — well, climbs, to be fair — in the wider region: there's the serious mountaineering proposition that is a summit assault on Mount Aspiring, and there's the pretty but demanding Cascade Saddle from the Matukituki Valley over into the Rees–Dart catchment.

Then there are easier walks, such as the climb to the Rob Roy Glacier from the Matukituki Valley, or the pleasant (if steep) scramble up to the summit of 1578 metre Mount Roy, just a couple of minutes' drive from Wanaka township. On the outskirts of town, there's the stroll to the top of 548 metre Mount Iron, giving grandstand views of the lake.

There are other popular walks on the lakefront, too. The most popular — and it's completely flat — is undoubtedly the Outlet Track, which begins about six kilometres from Wanaka township where the lake empties into the mighty Clutha River and follows the river downstream to Albert Town, five kilometres away. It was originally a narrow path used by anglers to get to their trout-fishing spots at Albert Town — and many of those plodding the path today carry rods and their catch. Otherwise, it's frequented by walkers, joggers, dog-walkers, skaters and mountain bikers.

For a couple of weeks during autumn, the Outlet Track becomes a breathtaking sight as the deciduous exotics lining the riverbank begin to cast off their autumn colours and the leaves of poplars and willows blanket the ground in swatches of gold, red and orange.

Kicking your way through here on a crisp, late afternoon, looking forward to a glass of Central Otago pinot noir by the fire at the end of it all . . . Oh, yes. Full-on lake effect.

PHOTO NEW ZEALAND

Visiting Lake Wanaka and Wanaka township in autumn is a must-do.

101 MUST-DO'S
FOR KIWIS

Puzzling World

Ever had that feeling they're messing with your mind? Well, at the Puzzling World of Stuart Landsborough, they most certainly are.

You'll know Puzzling World as soon as you see it, about a couple of kilometres outside Wanaka. The giveaway is the four towers, set at a decidedly rakish angle to gravity and to one another. Beyond them, there's the Leaning Tower of Wanaka, which is on a fairly distinctive tilt: 53 degrees compared with the just slightly skew-whiff Leaning Tower of Pisa, which departs from the vertical by a mere six degrees.

If you've ever wondered how all those laboratory rats you put through mazes in Psych 101 felt about it, here's your chance to find out. The Great Maze here has one and a half kilometres of passageways: it will take you half an hour if you manage to guess correctly at the bends, or an hour if you plod the whole way through. Alternatively, if you're suddenly seized by the fear that you're going to die in there, you can use the emergency doors and cheat your way out.

The really mind-bending stuff is in the various illusion rooms. The Hologram Hall is freaky enough, with lots of three-dimensional impossibilities apparently sharing the space. The Hall of Following Faces is another order of freakiness again, where 168 faces — many of whom you may recognise from telly and the movies — all seem to turn to look at you when you enter. Then they actually follow you as you move about. Let's get out of here.

From the outside, the Ames Forced Perspective Room looks benign enough, like a pretty ordinary kind of room, but once you're in there, you'll find funny things happening. Your sense of scale seems all up the pole — and indeed, the same devilishly clever techniques that were used to turn full-sized actors into hobbit-sized screen figures are at work here.

Tumbling Towers — hard to miss when entering the resort town of Wanaka.

PUZZLING WORLD

Then there's the Tilted House, where everything — floor, furniture, wall hangings and so on — are at a 15 degree tilt to the strictly level. Trouble is, your mind has spent so many years getting a handle on the horizontal, it's not about to give up now, and the corrections it makes lead to all sorts of perceptual discomfort.

Even the roof of the café forms a giant kaleidoscope, and when you go to powder your nose, you'll likely be tricked by a highly realistic mural into believing you've entered a Roman communal latrine. Perhaps you have. After all, nothing around here is quite what it seems.

PUZZLING WORLD

puzzlingworld.com
Wanaka N.Z.

Roman toilets — even visiting the amenities is a visual treat at Puzzling World.

The Blue Pools of Haast Pass

Maori knew about the glacial defile between the coastal flats of South Westland and the high tussock-land surrounding the southern lakes from their expeditions in search of pounamu, or the campaigns mounted by northern iwi to kick southern iwi butt, and vice versa.

The first European to cross what was to become Haast Pass did so in 1861, but it remained little more than a walking track for over a hundred years until a 19-year-long effort to extend State Highway 6 south from Westland was finally completed in late 1965. Dozens of bridges had to be built — there's more rivers and creeks than you can poke a surveyor's staff at in this part of the country — but anyone who cruises this road will agree that it was worth all the effort. It gives the motorist a grandstand view of the transition from the snowy mountains and tussock land surrounding Lake Wanaka through typical Westland rainforest to the coastal river flats. It's some of the loveliest scenery you'll ever see through a windscreen.

The trouble with roads, though, is that once you're on them, there's a temptation to grit your teeth, take a firmer grip on the steering wheel and press on past all the signposted attractions that flicker by. You mad blind fool, you.

Unless you're in too much of a hurry, you'll see a signpost near the Wanaka end of the Haast Pass road, just inside the boundary of the UNESCO World Heritage-listed Mount Aspiring National Park, that you'd do well to stop for. It points off into the bush where a short walk will bring you to one of those scenic masterpieces in which this little country of ours glories.

The Makarora River arises in the icefields of the Young Range and empties into Lake Wanaka. At the point in question, it flows lazily through a series of deep, rocky pools, faintly blued by their mineral content and studded with brown trout, fanning the current with their pectorals and sort of hanging there, taunting anglers who haven't brought their tackle.

The pools are reached by a gentle walk along a benched and graded gravel path, interspersed with boardwalks, which winds through beech forest to a swing bridge high above the river. From the centre of the span, you can marvel at the clarity of the water, eyeball the trout and enjoy a spectacular view of the Main Divide, serenaded all the while by tui and bellbird.

THIERRY HUET/PICTURESQUE

Take a gentle walk to the Blue Pools.

101 MUST-DO'S FOR KIWIS

Queenstown

Adventure Central in a country bursting at the seams with opportunities for excitement and really wild things is Queenstown. There's bungy jumping, jet-boating, rafting, canyoning, hang-gliding, parapenting, skydiving, skiing, snowboarding, tramping, mountaineering . . . you name it. For the less intrepid, there's golf or wine-tasting or sightseeing. And all of it takes place against the prettiest backdrop mountains, lakes and rivers can contrive.

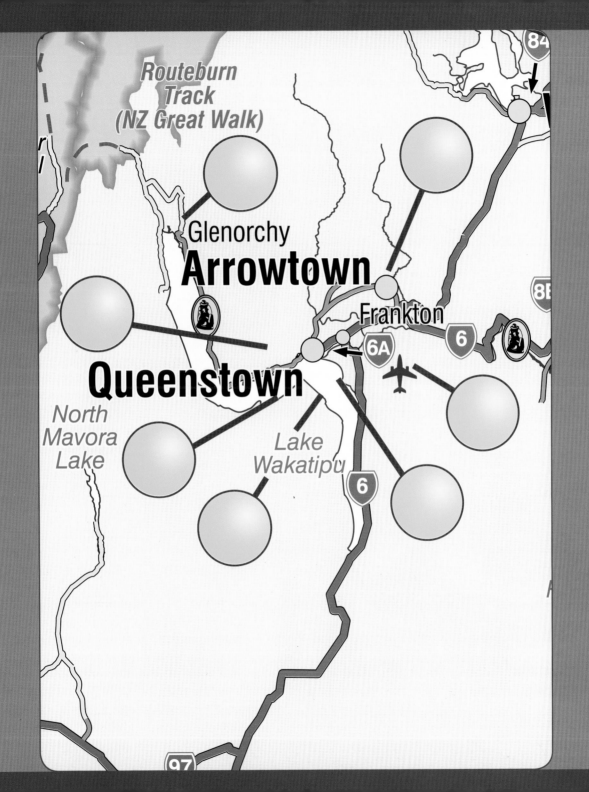

Arrowtown

Arrowtown with Millbrook Resort in the background.

BRIAN McCLOY

First, the Australian plate hit the Pacific plate with a bloody great crunch, shoving a bunch of the earth's crust upward in the big, jagged cockscomb we know as the Southern Alps. Then a succession of glaciers ground their way down the slopes, pounding the rock to powder. Then the ice melted, and the glaciers were replaced by rivers that carried the rock flour down to the lowlands and deposited it there. And finally, in 1862, millions of years after this whole process began, some joker swirled a bit of the Arrow River's alluvial grit around in his prospector's pan and swished the last fines out to reveal a nice, greasy-looking yellow crescent there.

The town's historic main street.

BRIAN McCLOY

With the discovery of gold in the bleak basin of the Arrow, it was all on for young and old. Hundreds of men who had upped sticks from the depleted fields of Victoria to chase 'the colour' in the tussock land around Gabriel's Gully the previous year now made the long trek to the site of the latest find. First, a tent city sprang up. Then, as the Arrow yielded up its riches, canvas was replaced by more permanent building materials, notably timber and the fine, flat local schist. A little town sprang up on the banks of the Arrow, laid out in the classic, frontier-town pattern with shop frontages flanking a main street barely wide enough for two carts to pass abreast. In a burst of inspiration for which the hard men of the goldfields were particularly noted, the settlement was named Arrowtown.

The beauty of Arrowtown is that it was built to last, and if you look carefully, you'll get some sense of what life was like for the miners. Some of the early workings are still visible, as are quite a few of the earliest permanent dwellings and commercial premises. Perhaps most poignant of all is the historic reserve where the restored dwellings of Chinese miners, who arrived to pick over the tailings of the claims already worked out by their European predecessors, have been preserved. For the full effect, come here in winter, try your hand at panning for gold in the bitter waters of the Arrow, then visit the Chinese settlement and imagine what it must have been like trying to get warm in a dirt-floored stone hut with a rag over the unglazed window and only a smoky fire for heat.

Boom followed bust in a cycle as relentless as the geological processes that shaped this area. First farming, then viticulture flourished in the gravelly soil; then the tourists came in numbers to rival the miners at the height of the rush. After all, Arrowtown's a pretty little spot, in all weathers and at any time of year.

I LOVE YOU NEW ZEALAND

What a quant little town. We have tried to find gold and every time my son finds fool's gold but who knows … This is the prettiest wee street I have seen and reminds me of an old settlement in Virginia, United States. Gorgeous. Try the bakery at the end of the street — they have the best pies in the South Island. Jacqui Clark

Ah Lum's store — part of the Arrowtown Chinese settlement.

DIDIER LIONNET AND ANNELISE SERRES

Glenorchy & Dart River

They'll tell you when you're standing at the confluence and delta of the Rees and Dart rivers that you're only 20 kilometres from Paradise.

Yeah, right, you'll mutter. Spare me the marketing hype.

No, really, they'll say. Just look at the map. There it is, right there: Paradise.

Due to its proximity to that fabled utopia, Glenorchy, at the head of the western arm of Lake Wakatipu, has been called the gateway to paradise. And in many ways, it's true — it's especially easy to believe if you can imagine that angels are manifested on earth as sandflies.

Glenorchy is a picturesque spot, backed by the craggy, snow-capped grandeur that is the interior of the Mount Aspiring National Park. And there's fun to be had in the area. Lots of it.

Trampers bound for some of the greatest walks in New Zealand depart from here: the Rees–Dart track itself, which performs a loop along the courses of these beautiful, glacier-fed waterways, lined with beech forest; the Greenstone and Caples tracks, which combine to form a similar circuit of the valleys of the Greenstone and Caples rivers; and, of course, the Routeburn, which is considered second only to the Milford Track as New Zealand's best tramping adventure.

If the very thought of hoofing it through

Floating down the Dart in a kayak.

the countryside makes you footsore, you're in luck. You can see the Dart River by jet-boat, ducking, weaving and swerving in the maze of channels and islets formed by the meandering braided river. And once up in the sheer-walled gorge in the wilds of Mount Aspiring National Park, you can choose to drift down the Dart in Funyaks — a very stable, very comfortable sort of short kayak.

However you choose to see it, by land or by water, you'll doubtless experience a fleeting sense of déjà vu: much of this incredible landscape, as with other particularly photogenic bits of our charismatic little country — was unrolled on the big screen as a backdrop to the cinematic marvel that was Peter Jackson's *Lord of the Rings* trilogy.

But if the big picture is more to your taste, you can get a panoramic view of it all from a helicopter or fixed-wing scenic flight from the Glenorchy airstrip: the rivers in their broad valleys and deep gorges, the soaring peaks and plunging bluffs, the snow and icefields all fall away beneath you.

Welcome to paradise. Any questions?

The scenic splendour can be viewed at speed.

DART RIVER SAFARIS

Golf in an Alpine Amphitheatre

In his poem 'High Country Weather', James K. Baxter writes about surrendering your anger to the skies.

This excellent advice applies to the fairway, or the bunker, or the rough. You've duffed a shot, say. Maybe you've duffed several. Okay, so you've managed to shift most of the sand from a bunker to the fairway without disturbing your ball, or you've hooked your drive gracefully into Lake Wakatipu. Or you've reached the green in two only to ten-putt the green. This is what you do: surrender your anger to the sky.

The sky in these parts will absorb a fair bit of anger. The ageless, snow-capped Remarkables preside over the area, aloof and indifferent alike to the vainglory of eagles and the ignominy of triple bogeys. Ripples spread out from the spot where your ball went into the lake, then the waters are immaculately still again, a reminder of how transitory are such trite considerations as par.

Kelvin Heights, the Queenstown Golf Club's course, is one of the prettiest of them all in a country famed the world over for its attractive golf courses. For those who find the proximity of water has a psychologically detrimental effect on their game, though, it's on the demanding side: the cunning and mildly sadistic designers have incorporated into many of the holes the 293 square kilometre water hazard that is Lake Wakatipu.

To limber up for the Kelvin Heights challenge, Queenstown Golf Club also maintains a nine-hole course and driving range at Frankton, next to the airport. Professional instructors are available there to help iron out the kinks in your swing.

Golfers visiting Queenstown will also want a round at the 18-hole course designed by Kiwi golfing legend Bob Charles for Millbrook Resort. Here too, serene and soothing views of the mountains are framed by tree, grass and sky whenever you fling your head back in exasperation.

Where else in the world can you start the day with a morning's skiing, follow it with a game of golf and round it off with a tall, cool drink in the 19th hole as the sunset gilds the snow-capped mountain ranges? Nowhere, that's where.

Take in the Remarkables and Lake Wakatipu as you walk between holes.

PHOTO NEW ZEALAND/JULIAN APSE

101 MUST-DO'S FOR KIWIS

TSS Earnslaw

Lake Wakatipu was once home to a number of steam-driven watercraft, in the days before road-building in the Lakes District really got underway. With the discovery of gold in the area, people suddenly acquired a powerful urge to get about, and steamers were the transport mode of choice, plying the lake from the main port of Kingston at the lake's southernmost extremity.

Once the gold rushes waned, the workaday business of supplying the farms of the district kept the Wakatipu steam flotilla in business. By the beginning of the twentieth century, the new gold rush — tourism — was getting underway. The volume of visitors to Lake Wakatipu was matched only by the volume of complaints about the standard of the accommodation on the cramped, crummy, stinky boats.

The government decided it was time a better class of steamer was laid on. It commissioned the vessel that was to become the *TSS Earnslaw* from Railways Department architect Hugh McRae. After a bit of a tussle over whether she ought to be a paddle or screw steamer, the job was handed over to Dunedin shipwrights John McGregor and Co, who had built similar vessels for the ferry service on Otago Harbour.

Once she had been put together on the Otago foreshore — a plaque commemorates the spot — the *Earnslaw* was disassembled and freighted kitset-fashion to Kingston, where she was put together again. The hull and decks were launched in February 1912, and her maiden voyage took place eight months later, on 18 October.

The *Earnslaw* has plied the sparkling waters of Lake Wakatipu ever since; her graceful, low-slung lines and plume of coal

smoke as much part of the scenery as the Remarkables.

The *Earnslaw* was a working girl in her early days, too, capable of carrying a mixed complement of cargo and passengers. In those days, tourists might sip their gin and tonics in the saloon, while up to 1500 sheep stomped the deck below nervously on their way to some station on Wakatipu's distant shore.

Not any more. You can use her as transport to Walter Peak and observe the working of a high-country sheep station, although the people have the pretty vessel all to themselves these days. The *Earnslaw* sails all year round and in all weathers, and there is no better way of seeing the lake than from her decks.

Though she's over 90 years old she looks as good as the day she was launched. The pure lake waters and clean alpine air have treated Queenstown's 'Lady of the Lake' very well.

Queenstown's 'Lady of the Lake'.

© REAL JOURNEYS

Queenstown Adventure

You feel pretty brave, standing there on the edge, your toes dangling in the void, the river moving lazily 100 metres below. Everything's a bit surreal, the sights and sounds all slightly heightened — the emerald river, the great, stony chasm of the gorge splitting the red-brown tussock, the mountains standing aloof against an equally pitiless sky, your mates making chicken noises and yelling 'Jump! Jump!'

You know in theory what you're supposed to do. You go on the count of three, right? And if you don't, they'll give you a gentle push.

Fine in theory. But in reality, the moment you topple beyond the point of no return, a little voice begins shrieking in your head: 'You bloody idiot! I spent all this time

🖳 The 102s

I hesitate to share this 'must-do' as part of the magic of The Nevis is that so few people know about it or go there. The Nevis is the highest public road in New Zealand — closed in winter and you need a four-wheel-drive to go right through — and they say that on a fine day you can see Mount Cook from on the top looking north over Lake Dunstan and Bannockburn to the mountains and lakes. Jackie Addenbrooke

keeping you alive and look what you go and do! Throw it all away!'

That's your survival instinct, overruled and despairing as you gain a wholly new and intimate appreciation of gravity. You gather speed, and all sensations become a blur as you prepare to watch the playback of your life that all the press about your final moments has led you to expect.

Then, just as it finally hits you that all is lost, you're heading in the opposite direction, jerked back into the air on the end of your giant rubber band. You will live! And you will live with something new inside you, an unforgettable glimpse into the infinite.

That's bungy jumping for you. It all began right here, in Queenstown, the bungy and — let's face it — adventure capital of the universe. A. J. Hackett was one of the first to risk it all leaping from

Queenstown — the bungy capital of the universe.

A.J. HACKETT/WWW.BUNGY.CO.NZ

a bridge, trusting only to his faith in the theoretical elastic qualities of the giant bungy cord he had devised. Now anyone can do it, but why they would want to do it anywhere other than in Queenstown, where the only thing that can match the thrill is the scenery, is anyone's guess.

Jet-boating also began in a commercial sense here, and you can do that too, if you're so compelled. You can go rafting on any one of a number of rapids, ranging from the restful to the ravening. You can take the jumping-to-certain-death thing to another level by trying tandem skydiving, or tandem hang-gliding or parapenting, or you can try the world's largest swing, 109 metres over the Shotover River.

The sky's the limit, and you get the impression it won't be long before the nutters down here push that, too — all for your adrenaline-charged pleasure.

Get your adrenaline pumping on the Shotover Jet.

101 MUST-DO'S FOR KIWIS

Winter Mountain Fun

Those who have enough trouble staying on their feet in skis or on a snowboard in optimal conditions will wonder why the hell you'd want to do it at night. That can only be because they haven't tried it.

The one place in New Zealand where you can ski or board at night — or, at least, where you can do it at night with the distinct advantage of artificial lighting to assist you — is Coronet Peak, one of the two superb fields right on Queenstown's doorstep. It is widely credited as being the place where the town's reputation as the winter fun capital of New Zealand began.

Few people find themselves out in the open air in the mountains at night, so quite apart from the skiing, just being on the slopes under a full moon (or crescent moon, or no moon) is an unusual and affecting experience.

And then to exit the chairlift and pause at the top of the slope, contemplating a piste transformed into pools of brilliant light and hollows of inky dark by the floodlights, is one right out of the box.

It takes a bit of adjustment, but once you learn to read the terrain, you're away. The huge floodlights give the whole thing a kind of big-match intensity, and the adrenaline seems to flow more freely than it does in the daytime.

Best of all, for the time being, the fact that you might be able to ski at night at all, let alone that you might be able to do it at Coronet Peak, hasn't yet occurred to the vast majority of the skiing public so the slopes are comparatively empty.

Night skiing is available at Coronet every Friday and Saturday night during the ski season until 9 p.m., conditions permitting. There's no better way to kick off a party weekend.

If, of course, you like to get to bed early, or you prefer to have the full benefit of daylight at your disposal on the slopes, then Coronet Peak remains one of New Zealand's premier skiing destinations. It has 280 hectares of skiable terrain, serviced by fast, comfortable lifts — and a multi-million dollar view of Lake Wakatipu and the Remarkables included in the lift-ticket price.

And if the sheer-looking snowfields of the Remarkables just get too tantalising, well, you can ski those, too.

Daytime, night-time, this mountain, that mountain. Don't say they don't aim to please down here.

MILES HOLDEN/CORONET PEAK

There's fun to be had for everyone on Coronet Peak.

101 MUST-DO'S FOR KIWIS

17

Waitaki & Dunedin

There's a number of peculiarities to peruse on your tour of the coastal route south to Dunedin. There's the otherworldly clutch of spherical boulders at Moeraki. There's the extraordinary and somehow incongruous opulence of Oamaru's white stone town centre. And then there's Dunedin itself, a city founded by dour churchmen and populated by hedonistic scarfies. Out there on the Otago Peninsula, there's a mainland albatross colony, and odd old Larnach Castle. Curiouser and curiouser . . .

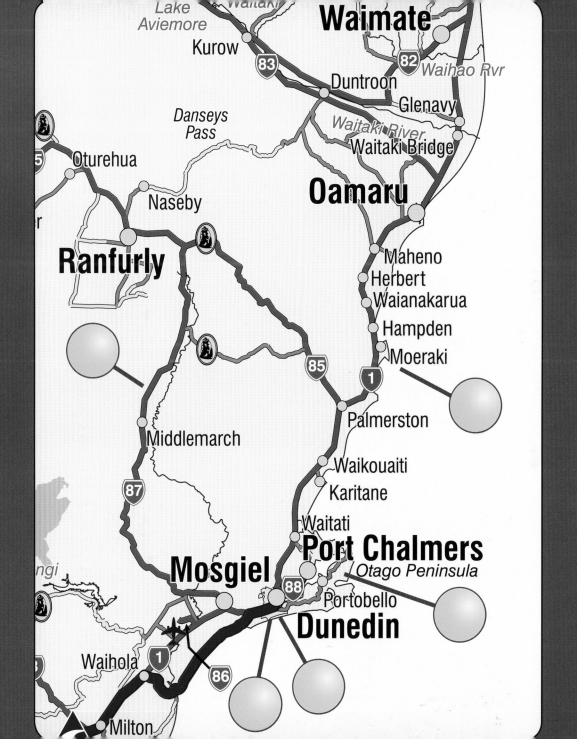

Dunedin City

TOURISM DUNEDIN

Robbie Burns stares out at the Edinburgh of the south.

Dunedin is an ancient name for Edinburgh, and the resemblance between our town and the Scottish one doesn't stop in the names. When their ship sailed into Otago Harbour the site of their future town must have warmed the cockles of the hearts of Dunedin's founders, Captain William Cargill and Thomas Burns, a nephew of that most Scots of Scotsmen, Robbie Burns.

Aye, they crooned. *Noo we're talkin'. The leaden skies. The cauld rocky foreshore. The drivin' sleet . . .*

They and the rest of the first settlers were Presbyterians, and thus they took to the rigours of the locale as readily as possums were elsewhere taking to the New Zealand rainforest. The Scots founded a flourishing town on the shores of the fine harbour, named Otago as a corruption of the Maori name, Otakou.

Flourishing was one thing, but they were staunchly disapproving when the gold rushes came along to enrich everybody and place Dunedin's entire population in danger of being able to live it up and have some fun for a change.

Which makes you wonder what those dour Free Churchmen would have made of present-day Dunedin, and in particular the non-stop bacchanalian round of the modern Otago University student's day.

They would have been gratified to see how much of the original, graceful, Gothic stone architecture has been preserved — First Church, Knox Church, Otago Boys' High School and the agreeably bleak Law Courts. They would have nodded approvingly when they learned the city's stadium, Carisbrook, was popularly known as the 'House of Pain', but they would have been concerned at how much the townsfolk seem to enjoy themselves in there. They would have declared themselves to be the last to cast aspersions on the fine products issuing from Mr Speight's brewery, but they would have deplored the sheer volume of it consumed in the course of scarfie revels. You can just picture the furrows on their brows, lit by the orange glow of burning sofas.

For those who don't share the narrow sensibilities of the city's founding fathers, the time to visit Dunedin is when the scarfies are in residence, as that's when the city is at its most vibrant. Drop in to The Cook, the Gardies or one of the other student haunts for a jug — if you dare. Or visit one of the many streets where palatial Edwardian residences now house flat-loads of scarfies. What you see may shock you — particularly if you can't abide cruelty to furniture — but it's all part of the atmosphere of the Edinburgh of the South. After all, Dunedin is a great spot, but it's the people — and especially the youth of the student body — that gives all that old stone its soul.

FAVOURITES

BEST ON A RAINY DAY
Dunedin Public Art Gallery, The Octagon

BEST RESTAURANT
Bell Pepper Blues, 474 Princes St

BEST VIEW
Rotary Park, off Highcliff Road as you drive onto the Otago Peninsula

BEST FISH AND CHIPS
Willowbank Takeaway, 995 George Street

TOURISM DUNEDIN

The imposing façade of Otago Boys' High School.

Moeraki Boulders

FAVOURITES

BEST DINING
Fleur's Place, 169 Haven Street

It just doesn't look natural. Just south of Oamaru, you've got this nice, sandy beach, right, but at a certain point there's a collection of perfectly round boulders, some smooth-skinned and intact, others fracturing along buttery veins of quartz, others eroded away to little more than piles of rubble.

The mystic appearance of the Moeraki boulders has drawn dreamers, artists, conspiracy theorists, crackpots and eccentrics for decades, and many of these folk have settled at the nearby clutch of cribs. It's a sleepy little place — which is, in fact, not far removed from the Maori name for it, 'moeraki' means 'long sleep'. But you don't really need a bunch of round rocks to make this a spot worth visiting.

Plenty of explanations for the boulders

Dinosaur eggs? Septarian concretions? You decide.

PHOTO NEW ZEALAND/ROB DRIESSEN

PHOTO NEW ZEALAND/MIKE HEYDON

The Moeraki boulders have an otherworldly quality.

have been advanced down the years. The local Maori tradition has it that the boulders are the flotsam cast from the wreck of the voyaging canoe Arai-te-uru, which came to grief on her way south in search of greenstone. A long, low reef at Shag Point, some 20 kilometres south of the boulder site, is said to be the wreck of the waka herself, and a nearby vertical rock formation the transfixed body of her commander.

They could, of course, be the marbles of the gods. Or dinosaur eggs. Or something to do with aliens — we all know alien artefacts when we see them. The most entertaining theory of all is that they are ballast stones once carried in the bilges of a great fleet of Chinese junks that discovered the world, including New Zealand, in the 15th century.

The least entertaining explanation,

on the other hand, is the one dreamed up by scientists. They'd have us believe that what we're looking at is a bunch of septarian concretions, which formed on the stony sea-floor some 60 million years ago. A piece of organic material, such as a dead animal, a lump of dinosaur dung or a bunch of plant matter, lies in the silt on the seafloor and forms a focal point for cementing minerals, which gradually build up into, in this case, a sphere. That's the concretion part. In septarian concretions, cracks in the sphere are invaded by other minerals — calcite in Moeraki's case. Long after the sea retreated, the boffins say, the concretions lay about embedded in mudstone, gradually emerging as the mudstone matrix eroded.

All of which just goes to show that when you boil it down, scientists are a bunch of killjoys.

101 MUST-DO'S FOR KIWIS

Otago Peninsula

TOURISM DUNEDIN

Larnach Castle perched high above Otago Harbour.

If ever you should tire of the splendours of Dunedin — preposterous though that proposition may sound — there's always the Otago Peninsula, extending from the city to the northeast, ending with the southern headland at the entrance to the harbour.

The coastline was an important source of kai moana for local Maori, and for as long as Dunedin has been settled by Europeans, the peninsula has been something of a local playground.

Otago University maintains a marine research facility at Portobello, and marine life is prolific. Large colonies of New Zealand fur seals, the rare Hooker's sea lion and populations of the equally rare yellow-eyed penguin are scattered along the Peninsula's shoreline. The Department of Conservation has constructed a number of hides close to the penguins' favoured landing points, and at the seaward extremity, Taiaroa Head, you'll find the world's only accessible mainland colony of northern royal albatross.

The Royal Albatross Centre, with its well-designed observatory, gets you as close to the birds as is comfortable for both you and them. Watching the birds, whether they're roosting, launching forth onto their 3.3 metre wingspan to scour the Southern Ocean for food, or returning to deliver the harvest of their long sojourn at sea to their young, you'll be struck by one thing. They're pretty damn big, these birds. Look one in the eye and you'll never be mean to a gull again.

The elevated spine of the peninsula sports an architectural curiosity in Larnach Castle. Financier and politician William James Mudie Larnarch is not remembered for much these days, besides the extraordinary folly he commissioned in 1871. Forget the yuppies of the 1980s, we had conspicuous consumers a hundred years before, and Larnach Castle is the ostentatious memorial of one of them.

The Englishmen who drafted it to Larnach's 'English manorial' specifications would have had difficulty believing that

their already overblown design finished up as it did — a Scots-style stone edifice adorned with every frill of masonry and joinery that Larnach's not inconsiderable budget could contrive. Larnach was fond of calling his residence 'The Camp', to commemorate the years he and his family spent camping in various of the building's 43 rooms as tradesmen came and went and pottered about with the details.

Whether the castle is tasteful is questionable, but set as it is amid park-like gardens, fascinating and unfamiliar in this landscape it most certainly is.

TOURISM DUNEDIN

One of the harbour's rare residents, a yellow-eyed penguin.

101 MUST-DO'S FOR KIWIS

Fiordland

The words 'untouched' and 'unspoiled' are overused these days, but not when it comes to Fiordland. Rugged, remote and for the most part pretty inhospitable, it tolerates only temporary human incursions, and rewards them handsomely. The tramping tracks here — the Milford, Routeburn, Kepler, Dusky and Hollyford — are world-renowned wilderness experiences. The scenic beauty of the fiords themselves, including Milford and Doubtful sounds, are gob-smacking.

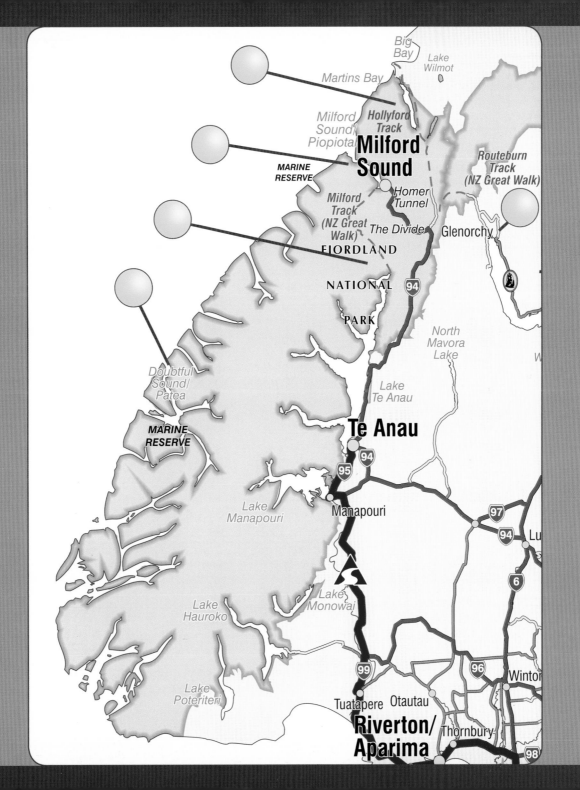

Doubtful Sound

DESTINATION FIORDLAND/TRACY TIBBLES

The most obviously dubious aspect of Doubtful Sound is its name because as most people know, it's actually a fiord, carved from the mountains by the action of a glacier long since gone the way of an icecream in high summer. It's bigger than Milford Sound, longer and covers far more area.

James Cook named the entrance to the sound Doubtful Harbour when, after noting that it afforded a 'very snug' anchorage, he wondered whether the howling nor'westerlies would ever let him out again if he ventured in.

Most visitors these days approach Doubtful Sound by land — following the launch trip across Lake Manapouri from Pearl Harbour to West Arm — joining an orphaned road where tour coaches have been strategically located to conduct you over the last few kilometres to Doubtful Sound itself.

On the way, you'll stop to enjoy the amazing view over the upper reaches of the waterway from Wilmot Pass, one of the most photographed outlooks in the country, weather permitting. This is Fiordland after all, where it's not uncommon for six or seven metres of rain to fall in a good year — enough to fill the deep end of a diving pool.

You'll join your boat at Deep Cove, and venture past the stunning Helena Falls on your way out to the islets where the sound joins the sea. On the way, you'll more than likely share the water with seals or a pod of dolphins, both of which abound here. Everything you hear — the thunder of the cataract, the throb of the launch's engines, the birdsong from the beech forest clinging to the sheer walls of the sound, the gasp of a surfacing bottlenose dolphin, the cheery commentary of your guide, the clatter of camera shutters — is laid over the cathedral-like silence, the true sound of the sound, as it were.

At the sound's entrance, the lake-like serenity changes to the brooding, rugged drama of the Tasman Sea.

If, of course, you want to minimise the risk of having the tall bits of the sound obscured by misty rain clouds, the best thing to do is join an overnight cruise in the area. You won't regret it. After all, with the sole exception of Captain James Cook, no one who visits this place is in a hurry to get away.

Take a boat trip among the islets of Doubtful Sound and you are likely to come across seals and dolphins.

Enjoy the sound
of silence.

223

101 MUST-DO'S
FOR KIWIS

Fiordland National Park

They may nibble at its margins, but Fiordland National Park will always defy the developers and the spoilers. To start with, there's plenty of it — 1.2 million hectares, to be precise — and it's pretty rugged terrain at that, accessible largely by air or laborious leg-work.

The township of Te Anau nestled on the banks of Lake Te Anau.

Some of the particular attractions of the park are must-dos in their own right: Doubtful and Milford sounds and the Hollyford Track. But these leave much of the Fiordland area untouched.

Once you've experienced the wonders of the park from the ground, whether by

DESTINATION FIORDLAND/GRAHAM DAINTY

driving through to Milford Sound or joining a Doubtful Sound excursion, or by walking one of the great tracks in the area such as the Milford, the Routeburn, the Hollyford or, for the experienced, the Dusky, the very best way to experience Fiordland is by air.

The lofty peaks fall away beneath you, with great swooping plunges of snow and ice fall, bluff and crag, scree and shingle sloping down to the rivers in their stony beds. The fiords on the coast lie blue amongst the daunting fastness of the rainforest, and the lakes on the eastern margin mark the park's boundary with the golden tussock-land of Central Otago.

There are, of course, other more exotic experiences to be had in the remote reaches of Fiordland National Park. There's back-country fishing, and gold and greenstone fossicking to be done. There's hunting, with several species of deer and rumours of a population of moose surviving since they were released on the coast 100-odd years ago. Or there's wilderness surfing — staging an aerial assault by chartered plane on the break at Big Bay.

It's Wilderness Central, and it's waiting for you, if you're game.

I LOVE YOU NEW ZEALAND

The most exciting month ever spent tramping the Hollyford, Routeburn, Rees and Dart Tracks. Awesome scenery, magic views and the best way to get back to nature.
Doreen Gardner

FAVOURITES

BEST FREE STUFF
See takahe and other birds at the Te Anau Wildlife Centre

BEST VIEW
The viewing point at Ramparts Road overlooking Te Anau township and lake

BEST ON A RAINY DAY
Fiordland Cinema, The Lane

Take a scenic flight over Fiordland National Park.

DESTINATION FIORDLAND

Hollyford Valley

Less popular than the nearby Milford and Routeburn tracks, the Hollyford Track is nonetheless one of the South Island's great tramping experiences. It follows the course of the longest valley in Fiordland National Park from the Darran Mountains out to remote and beautiful Martin's Bay.

It can be done either in style, with guides and private lodge accommodation, or under your own steam, staying at the Department of Conservation's excellent huts. Unusually for Fiordland tracks, it has no alpine passes to contend with, but that's not to say it's easy.

Walk the Hidden Falls Creek Swing Bridge in the Hollyford Valley.

HOLLYFORD TRACK WWW.HOLLYFORDTRACK.COM

The track begins at the end of a road off State Highway 94, from Te Anau to Milford. It takes around four days to reach Martin's Bay, depending how hard you want to push it and whether you avail yourself of the jet-boat service that cuts out the most demanding section of the track.

Most of the walk is comparatively easy, following the flats alongside the Hollyford River. The highest point on the track, which you strike on the second day's walk, is a steady rather than a steep climb, and the effort is rewarded with views of Mount Madeline and, further south, Fiordland's highest peak, the 2746 metre Mount Tutoko. There are two picturesque waterfalls along the way, a huge swing-bridge over Pykes River, a pretty tract of southern podocarp forest and the two lakes you encounter on your way — lakes Alabaster and McKerrow — boast more than passable trout fishing.

At Lake McKerrow, you have a choice of transport modes. You can continue to hoof it, or you can catch a ride on a jet-boat the length of the lake, thus skipping what has been called 'the most exhausting non-alpine day's walk in New Zealand', evocatively named the Demon Trail.

The Hollyford Track ends at Martin's Bay, where you will be welcomed by the opportunity to get up close to a big seal colony and a penguin rookery.

The return journey can be accomplished via Big Bay and Lake Alabaster (another four to five days' walk), by turning around and retracing your steps up the Hollyford, or by catching a ride on a plane or helicopter. Try watching all that terrain you've so laboriously covered in days of footsore toil roll away beneath you in a matter of minutes and see if you don't have a whole new respect for technology.

HOLLYFORD TRACK WWW.HOLLYFORDTRACK.COM

HOLLYFORD TRACK WWW.HOLLYFORDTRACK.COM

Journey into the most beautiful valley in New Zealand.

101 MUST-DO'S FOR KIWIS

Mitre Peak & Milford Sound

Many visitors to Fiordland don't believe in Mitre Peak. The tour guide on their launch trip points to a bluff rising vertically into the curtain of low cloud and announces that if only it were clear, that's where the majestic vista familiar to consumers of postcards the world over could be seen.

Yeah, right, the sceptics mutter, and depart darkly suspecting that the pictures of the great triangular peak rising from its inverse in the mirror-smooth waters of the sound were cleverly put together in a suite of image-manipulation software.

But even those who miss out on seeing the area's A-list celebrity peak won't leave Milford Sound disappointed. When you visit in the rain — and with rain falling on over 200 days out of 365, there's a pretty high chance you will — you'll see it with all the taps turned on, and that's a sight to behold. Over 100 waterfalls start gushing from the sheer walls of the sound. The largest of these, Stirling Falls, crashes 146 metres from the rocky cleft from which it issues into the glassy sea.

The sound — okay, for the pedants, it's really a fiord — is the sight for sore eyes that greets walkers emerging from the Milford Track, but it can be reached by road via the Homer Tunnel and by air as well. To appreciate it fully, you need to get out on the water, whether on one of the many cruises available, or in a kayak. The intrepid can join a guided scuba party, and

Join the *Milford Mariner* on a tour of the sound.

I LOVE YOU NEW ZEALAND

Unbelievably beautiful, in any weather. A truly magic place, the gem of our lovely country.
Ernie Stevenson

be rewarded with a close-up look at black coral. This coral usually occurs well below the depths to which recreational divers can safely go, but at Milford a layer of tannin-rich fresh water sits atop the seawater, re-creating the twilight of the abyss in the shallows. Or you can cheat: anyone who can handle a descent of the spiral staircase at the Milford Sound marine observatory can get the same view.

Many of the other peaks crowding to the margins of the long waterway nudge 2,000 metres. The highest of Mitre Peak's five summits rears 1683 metres from the water, and the water itself at its deepest point is 420 metres straight down. But in the end, the numbers mean nothing. The ineffable scale and grandeur of this landscape has to be experienced to be believed. If Mitre Peak does deign to reveal itself on the day of your visit, prepare to have your flabber well and truly gasted.

Magnificent Mitre Peak in a reflective mood.

Central Otago

T he great arid basin of the Maniototo defies description. It's an empty landscape, alternating between bitter winters and scorching summers, all beneath the biggest sky in New Zealand. For all its emptiness and solitude, it offers some unique experiences: curling, for heaven's sake, and the fantastic Central Otago Rail Trail. It's littered with history, and the hospitality is as warm as the winters are frigid.

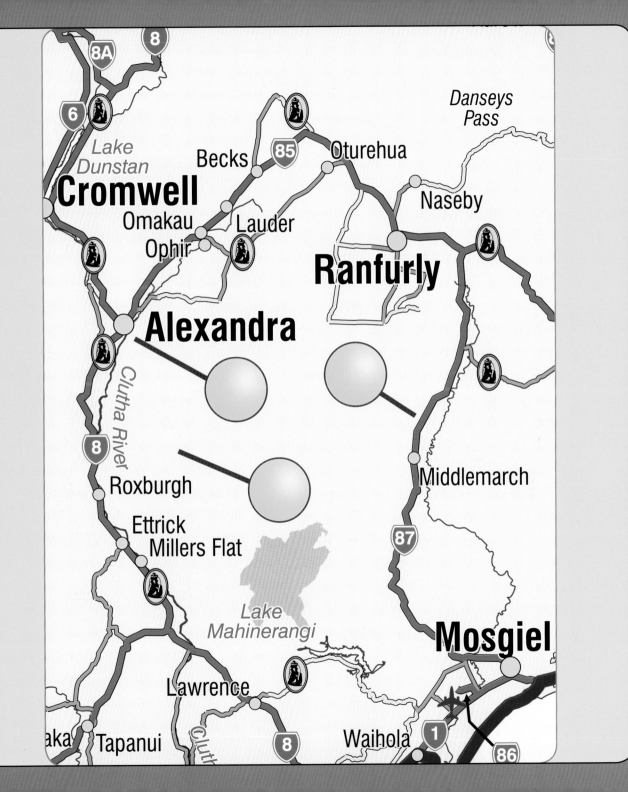

Central Otago Curling

No one really knows where the peculiar sport of curling originated, but there's no doubt that it was the Scots who took it to their heart, kept it there when they migrated to New Zealand, just in case they found climate and terrain suitable for play.

Well, it's hard to imagine a better landscape, or a better climate, than the Maniototo Plain with its hard frosts and bitter winters.

The father of New Zealand curling, Thomas Callender, founded the first club — where else but in Dunedin — in the 1870s, and the first reported game in the Maniototo took place on 6 July, 1878. Then, as now, an ancient form of the game is played here that is all but forgotten in the rest of the curling world.

In common with the kind of curling that has been an official Olympic sport since the 1998 Nagano Winter Olympics, players of 'crampit curling' deliver 20-kilogram granite stones from one end of an ice rink (or 'sheet') toward a target (the 'tee', or 'house') at the other. Players from opposing teams take turns doing this, with the closest stones to the target scoring points for their team. The rules are not unlike lawn bowls, even if the language is rather different — you'll often hear players encouraging one another to 'crack the egg'.

Unlike Olympic curling, where the players set their stones in motion from down on one knee, gaining

I LOVE YOU NEW ZEALAND

A wicked sport anyone can participate in! The best part: mulled wine, whisky and tall tales in front of the fire afterwards. Rebecca Lilley

purchase with their toes in holes ('hacks') in the ice, crampit curlers deliver them from a standing position on a metal plate called a crampit. In all forms of the game, team-mates of the player who has delivered the stone accompany it down the rink, madly 'sooping' the ice — sweeping it with brooms to polish away ice crystals that slow its progress. It's a strange ritual to the uninitiated.

Don't be afraid to give curling a go. Like all enthusiasts of niche activities, curlers are only too happy to welcome newcomers to the sport. And as you don't actually need to lift the stone, anyone can play.

What's more, you don't have to wait for the big freeze needed for a 'bonspiel' (or tournament) to be called, you can play year round. The picturesque little town of Naseby, which aspires to be the 'ice capital' of New Zealand, has just opened an Olympic-standard curling rink.

Best of all, a curling tournament traditionally finishes with a plate of beef and greens washed down with whisky. Now we're talking. Good curling to ye!

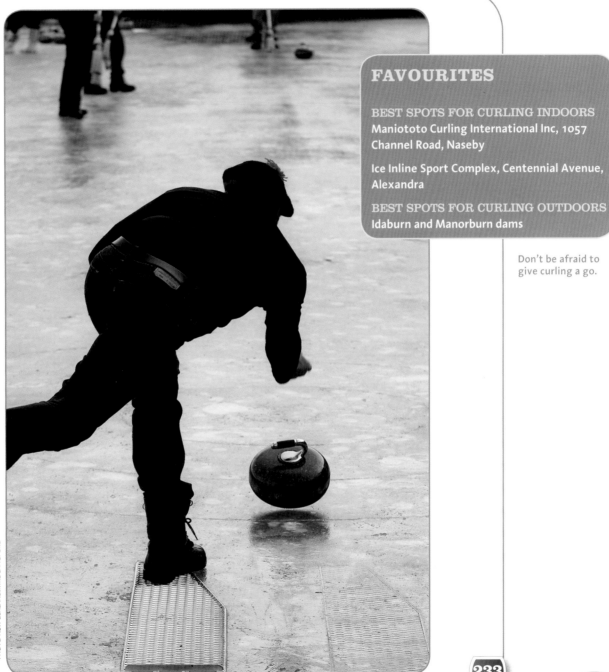

PHOTO NEW ZEALAND/MIKE LANGFORD

FAVOURITES

BEST SPOTS FOR CURLING INDOORS
Maniototo Curling International Inc, 1057
Channel Road, Naseby

Ice Inline Sport Complex, Centennial Avenue,
Alexandra

BEST SPOTS FOR CURLING OUTDOORS
Idaburn and Manorburn dams

Don't be afraid to
give curling a go.

Otago Rail Experience

Rail was once meant to be the backbone of the New Zealand economy. In the late 1800s, the Premier Sir Julius Vogel imagined we would one day see every farm, mill and mine within easy reach of a railhead, with branch lines feeding the North and South Island Main Trunk lines.

True to this plan, the sheep runs of Central Otago once fed their produce out to the export ports of the coast via the 152 kilometre Central Otago line, which connected with a service through the Taieri Gorge to Dunedin. There were passenger services too but, as a result of improved road access to the area, these were discontinued in 1976. Restrictions on carrying farm produce by road kept the line busy though. These restrictions were lifted

Dunedin's grandiose railway station.

TOURISM CENTRAL OTAGO

in 1983 but by then the construction of the Clyde Dam was well under way. The Central Otago line gained a reprieve as it was used to carry freight to the dam's massive building site. The opening of the dam was followed by the closure of the railway line in 1990.

Happily, though, the route still serves sightseers. You can enjoy a spectacular day-trip by train up the Taieri Gorge, courtesy of the Otago Excursion Train Trust. Or you can use the Taieri Gorge Railway to transport you to the start of your traverse of the Central Otago Rail Trail.

You board the Taieri Gorge excursion trains at Dunedin's fabulously blowsy railway station. Opened in 1906, it's not hard to see why this elaborate piece of architecture earned for its designer the nickname 'Gingerbread'.

The railway follows the coast for a few kilometres then strikes inland up the rugged, rocky course of the Taieri River. The climb to Central Otago takes you across stone and wrought-iron bridges, and past little iron railwaymen's huts — all testament to the sheer physical hardship endured by those who drove the rails through.

Middlemarch marks the end of the line. From here, the tracks have been lifted and the route regraded with crushed rock, suitable for cyclists, pedestrians and horseriders. It's 150 kilometres: a long way to pedal, you might think, when you haven't been on a bike for years. But it can be tackled in three or four leisurely days, and your overnight, lunch and comfort stops can all be scheduled to take place at the region's legendary little pubs. There's nothing like an ice-cold Speight's or two to take your mind off the chafing and the saddle-soreness.

And then there's the scenery. When you look about you, it seems it can't possibly have existed before Grahame Sydney painted it. There's a desolate grandeur to this countryside, whether it's under snow or the tussock is dressed in its summer and autumn golds, and it's all presided over by the biggest sky in New Zealand.

The tracks from Middlemarch to Clyde have been regraded so they are perfect for cyclists, but beware of saddle-soreness.

TOURISM CENTRAL OTAGO

Southland

Whether Bluff is your southernmost destination or you venture further across Foveaux Strait to Stewart Island, pleasures await you in the deep south. The Catlins coast between Dunedin and Invercargill is one of the loveliest drives in New Zealand, with plenty of opportunities to linger. Stewart Island is an untouched reach of paradise; the dawn chorus on the open wildlife sanctuary of Ulva Island is a glimpse of old New Zealand, and must be heard to be believed.

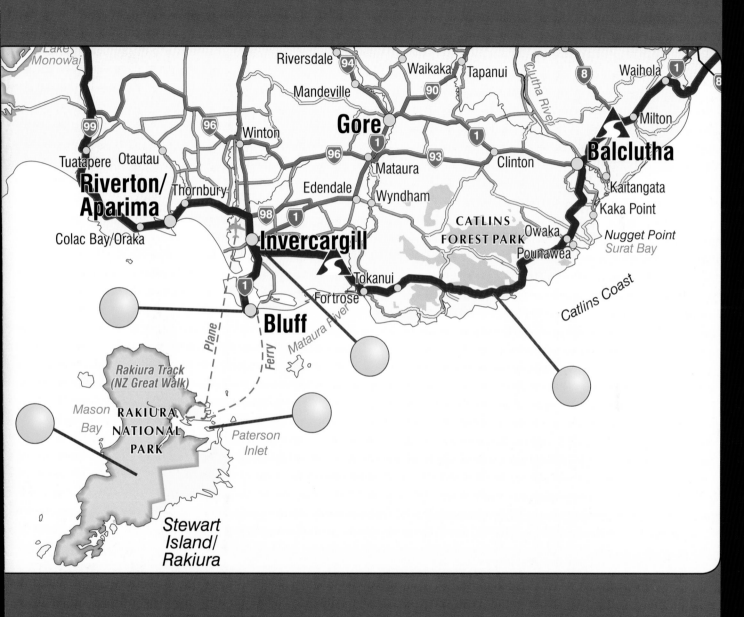

Southern Scenic Route

If you get as far south as Te Anau, it'd be rude not to keep going and have a look at the deep south, don't you reckon?

Beyond Te Anau, you can either take a detour off State Highway 94 to visit Manapouri (and Doubtful Sound beyond). From there you can follow the web of secondary roads into the wilds of Southland to Tuatapere and the little fishing town of Riverton.

Or you can stick with State Highway 94, south to Winton and the southernmost city in the world, Invercargill. Either way, you'll want to press on through Invercargill to Bluff, climb the hill and contemplate the Southern Ocean from the New Zealand mainland's most southerly point.

After that head out around the coast to 'the Catlins', as it's known in this part of the world, where they pronounce 'fur seal' as though there are four Rs in 'fur'. And fur seals there assuredly are, along with Hooker's sea lions, yellow-eyed penguins and Hector's dolphins, along with immaculate white-sand beaches (many receiving New Zealand's biggest surfable waves on their day), tracts of native bush, rivers, lakes and waterfalls.

A popular tourist destination is Curio

Bay, where you can walk among the visible remnants of a 180 million-year-old petrified forest. At dusk the yellow-eyed penguins haul out and spend the night among the boulders at the head of the beach.

Curio Bay is on the western headland of Porpoise Bay, where pods of little Hector's dolphins frequently swim within spitting distance of shore. (Not that they spit, of course, and nor should you.) Seals and endangered Hooker's sea lions lumber up the beaches of this coastline, too, to bask in the southern sunshine.

Further round, you can make a short detour out to Nugget Point, where there's a lighthouse perched on a headland above a set of small, weather-beaten islets. The views from here are well worth a look,

southwest along the south coast, northeast across Molyneux Bay towards the Otago Peninsula in the misty distance. There's a gannet colony here, and besides the usual sea lions and seals, you may spot the odd sea elephant, too.

All the way around the Catlins road, there are side-trips of scenic and historical significance. Just north of Papatowai, you can visit Purakaunui Falls, one of the most photographed cataracts in New Zealand.

From Kaka Point, where the density of cribs increases, you're out of the remote southern leg of the circuit and on the road to Dunedin — back to civilisation of a kind.

Explore Curio Bay and see the remnants of a petrified forest.

VENTURE SOUTHLAND TOURISM

Stewart Island

VENTURE SOUTHLAND TOURISM

There are over 220 kilometres of track to be tramped on Stewart Island.

As you go south, twilight lengthens. By the time you've crossed Foveaux Strait and arrived at Halfmoon Bay, the principal settlement on the southernmost of New Zealand's three main islands, Stewart Island, sunsets and sunrises stretch into smouldering pyrotechnic displays. This is why the Maori knew Stewart Island as Rakiura — 'land of the glowing sky' — although it's also a splendid vantage from which to see the southern lights, the aurora australis, too.

Captain James Cook made one of his rare mistakes when charting Stewart Island. He spied it from afar, but didn't pick it for an island, supposing Foveaux Strait to be the entrance to a big bay. (This sort of made up for his other boo-boo, turning

Banks Peninsula into an island.) It was left to Captain William Stewart, a seadog of murky repute who visited New Zealand waters three decades after Cook, to fill the strait with water. For that, he got the newly recognised island named after him.

The great thing about Stewart Island from the present-day perspective is that down the years no one really found much point settling there. Sporadic rushes on the island's seals, whales, gold, tin and fish have caused the occasional spike in the resident population, but even today, it's just over 400 strong. The failure of all these attempts to get a boom going has meant that Stewart Island has been passed down to us more or less unspoilt, and much of its 157,000 hectares now forms the Rakiura National Park.

Visitors from the north will immediately notice the profusion of birdlife. Species that are rare outside bird sanctuaries further north — such as kaka and kiwi — are comparatively plentiful here. Indeed, most visitors will get to see a kiwi in the wild if they wish, whether in the course of their own nocturnal explorations, or as a member

of a dedicated 'spotting' party.

There's plenty of superb tramping to be done in the national park, with over 220 kilometres of tracks maintained throughout. The Rakiura Track, which was opened a mere 20 years ago, is one of New Zealand's Great Walks. It takes three days to traverse, during which time you'll see few other souls, plenty of birds, a diverse landscape with rocky ridges and bluffs soaring clear of the rainforest, and heaps and heaps of mud. Longer tramps are available, and for the less energetic, there are cruises and, of course, the option of just kicking back and watching the sunset.

Sunset over Stewart Island — 'land of the glowing sky'.

VENTURE SOUTHLAND TOURISM

FAVOURITES

BEST ALL-ROUND ENTERTAINMENT
Charliez Pizzeria and Rakiura Theatre,
10 Main Rd, Halfmoon Bay

BEST TRIP
West coast to east coast, Stewart Island Flights

BEST WINING AND DINING
South Sea Hotel, Halfmoon Bay

I LOVE YOU NEW ZEALAND

Awesome fishing experience, massive blue cod, no real skill needed, only a sharp hook and strong arms.
Malcolm Carrod

Ulva Island

There's something disturbingly anatomical about Ulva Island's name, so it probably comes as something of a relief to learn it was named after a Scottish island of the same name by surveyors in the 1800s.

Ulva Island is situated in Paterson Inlet, the main bay on Stewart Island, and can be reached by a short boat trip from Halfmoon Bay or Golden Bay.

And the trip is well worth the effort. Ulva Island is administered by the Department of Conservation as an 'open sanctuary' — a sanctuary you can visit — and is a birdwatchers' paradise.

The 266 hectare Ulva was first designated a wildlife sanctuary in 1899, but it wasn't until 1997 that the last rat was hunted down and dispatched, and the island was declared officially predator-free. Since then, a number of rare species have been re-introduced, including the South Island saddleback, the Stewart Island robin and a threatened species of skink.

Other bird species thrive, too: weka, kiwi, kereru, kaka, kakariki, tomtit, fantail, rifleman, tui and bellbird — and all twitter, shriek and flute about you as you walk the island's tracks.

Ulva Island is home to many native birds including the kiwi and kaka (opposite).

VENTURE SOUTHLAND TOURISM

Rare plants also flourish, including two, the lanternberry and the tmsepteris, which grew in Gondwanaland before the dinosaurs walked the earth and anyone could be sure where the vowels in their names should go. Again, other species present on the mainland can be seen at their best on Ulva Island — rimu, rata, totara and miro in the canopy and an impenetrably dense understorey show what the New Zealand bush can look like when it isn't logged and browsed to bits.

There are three main walking tracks to explore on the island. They meander between Post Office Cove, Sydney Cove, Boulder Beach and West End Beach, providing the chance to see some of the rarest plants in the world. Dawn's the best time to visit, because that's when the birds pump up the volume. It's a sound you won't easily forget — the dawn chorus as Tane intended. The mainland mornings will seem strangely quiet forever after.

VENTURE SOUTHLAND TOURISM

In a country where we all live so close to nature, it's little wonder we harbour a national passion for getting back to it. Whether you do it in comparative style — in a motor home or caravan with all mod-cons — or whether you do it with tent, groundsheet and sleeping bag, camping is one of the best ways there is to see the out-of-the way bits of our country.

Most holiday destinations have a campground or motor camp. You'll generally find a spot where, for a few bucks, you can pitch a tent and use the communal facilities for cooking and ablutions. Most motor camps have cabin-style accommodation or on-site caravans for hire for those who wish to rough it in a slightly more refined fashion.

The Department of Conservation administers a network of 235 campsites, all strategically located to place you within easy reach or eyeshot of the splendours of our national parks and recreation reserves. The facilities at these range from the basic — the cold-water camps at some of our prettiest beaches, for example, where the showers are (as the name suggests) cold and the toilets are of the composting or long-drop type — to the comparatively luxurious, where there are flush toilets, barbecue facilities and a friendly ranger to keep order.

Whole generations of New Zealanders go misty-eyed when the lid is removed from a bottle of insect repellent, remembering camping holidays from days gone by. The scent of crushed kikuyu grass sparks instant nostalgia for all those mornings you woke at sunrise, as the sun's first rays set the interior temperature of your tent soaring. And if you somehow reproduce the rattle of rain on canvas, you evoke powerful memories of bygone summers. For although it's a fact that the mass pitching of tents is one of the more effective rain-making rituals known to humanity, it's also true that a dash of adversity makes the camping experience more memorable.

You know you're a Kiwi when you've been inducted into the brotherhood or sisterhood of those who know how to spark up a Primus or a gas stove, and have learned the futility of trying to dodge the plume of smoke from a campfire. For while fires are no longer allowed at formal campsites in most of the North Island, you can still have a decent blaze in campgrounds around the South Island.

After all, the stars seen through eyes smarting from woodsmoke is the preferred Kiwi view of the night sky.

© REAL JOURNEYS

Pitch a tent
and chill out at
Landsborough in
the South Island.

245

North Island

Art Deco Weekend: Napier, February

Eighteen years after the first Art Deco Weekend was held in Napier — a low-key, two-day affair — the festivities now last for five days, with some events spanning a fortnight. Held on the third weekend of February, the Brebner Print Art Deco Weekend is, loosely speaking, a celebration of art deco architecture. The Hawke's Bay region is generously endowed with examples of art deco thanks to the 1931 earthquake, which wiped the slate clean just in time for everything to be rebuilt in the fashion of the day.

The festivities have a thirties theme — the music is ragtime, the clothes are zoot suits, the women are flappers and the cars are fantastic. There are nearly 60 events, including a Great Gatsby Picnic, a Bathing Belle Competition and the Depression Dinner. You can experience a bi-plane ride, and while the guided walks around Napier's premier art deco sites are available at any time of year, the festival provides the perfect excuse to join one.

Auckland Anniversary Day Regatta/Auckland Harbour Festival: Auckland, January

Auckland's Anniversary Day Regatta has always been a spectacular sight, putting the 'sails' in the City of Sails. Viewing the profusion of craft of all shapes and sizes thronging the Waitemata, you can't help but wonder where all these boats have come from.

From windsurfers and P-classes to square-rigged five-masters, you'll see just about anything that floats and flies a scrap of canvas out there having a go. The regatta includes racing for all classes, and includes a classic yacht regatta — where the grand old kauri-hulled, timber-sparred gaffers grace the harbour, as some have for nigh on 100 years — and the concluding races in a five-day international match-racing series.

You can watch from many vantage points around the harbour, particularly Devonport's North Head, but the second best view is from a charter boat out on the water. The best view of all, of course, is from the deck of a competing yacht.

The regatta itself forms the centrepiece of the wider Auckland Harbour Festival, which also features fireworks displays, live local and international bands, street theatre and fun rides.

Big Day Out: Auckland, January

It wasn't so long ago that the Big Day Out used to approach New Zealand without ever quite reaching it, like a comet. The nearest point in its orbit to our shores was Sydney, and such was the line-up of bands it attracted that Kiwis would make the pilgrimage across the ditch to catch it. Now its annual appearance in our musical heavens is even more eagerly awaited, because the Big Day Out makes it to Auckland every January.

One ticket gives you access to the Mount Smart arena, and within you have a choice of several stages and marquees each specialising in a certain genre. You can appreciate the guitar virtuosity of metal and grunge outfits from heaving sweating mosh pits, or zone out to samples and drops in the dance tent, or pull your hoodie low and breakdance to a hip hop crew, according to your taste.

The headline acts each year are A-list international heavyweights: in 2006, the Big Day Out offered New Zealanders the only chance they'll ever have to see The White Stripes, Iggy Pop and the Stooges and Franz Ferdinand on the same bill.

The only trouble is that you're spoiled for choice. How to catch all the acts at once? Roll on cloning.

Christmas in the Park, Auckland Domain: Auckland, December

A balmy evening in the Auckland Domain is always good for a picnic. And spreading a blanket on the grass, laying out the contents of your hamper and chillybin of a balmy evening in December with 199,999 others for Christmas in the Park is one of the chief pleasures of life in the Queen City.

Top New Zealand singers and an array of celebrities take turns to serenade the crowd with carols, and the whole thing is capped off with a spectacular fireworks display. It's all pretty civilised, sitting there with a sav blanc and a chicken wing in the twilight listening to the music. It gets you in the mood for Christmas and into the swing of summer.

Coromandel Beach Hop: Whangamata, April

Each April, American Graffiti gets sprayed, figuratively speaking, all over Whangamata on the east coast of Coromandel Peninsula. Everyone who's ever grown a sideburn will be there — 60,000 of them in 2005. Classic cars, their brightwork sparkling like water, and hot rods, fantasies of paint and chrome and lower than a scared cat, converge on the town — over 1500 of them, at the last count. Local restaurants deck themselves out as fifties diners and milk bars, and rock'n'roll bands pomade their quiffs, adjust their tuxedos, strap their guitars on their chests and shake it up, do the twist and generally get down. Surfers pull out their big Mals for the occasion, hanging ten in the slick of brylcreem out there in Whangamata's beautiful bay.

There's also a sixties fashion show, a nostalgic golf competition, drive-in movies, a low-brow art competition and a market.

The most fun to be had since Elvis left the building.

Ellerslie Flower Show: Auckland, November

It's kind of hard to believe that the nationally famous event that is the Ellerslie International Flower Show started out as a fundraiser for the Rotary Club. Since its modest beginnings, it's, er, bloomed: it's now the largest show of its type in the southern hemisphere and has grown way too big for its former venue, Ellerslie Racecourse. These days, it's based at the Auckland Regional Botanic Gardens in Manurewa. Held over five days, it sprawls over five and a half hectares, and features exhibitions from top designers, florists, gardeners and horticulturalists.

Several feature gardens are also on show, including winners from previous Ellerslie Flower Shows and local entries to international garden spectaculars such as the Chelsea Flower Show. There's also entertainment, food and drink available. Blooming good fun.

Endless Summer Festival: Whangarei, March

It's not bad in the winterless north at any time of year, but summer in Whangarei is spectacular.

Once a dreary little town on the muddy upper reaches of the tidal harbour, Whangarei has been transformed, ever since the town basin area was given over to cafés and bars instead of bait sheds and port buildings. Now there's somewhere to sit and enjoy the sunshine.

The Endless Summer Festival fills the long, sun-drenched days and the warm summer evenings with dance, theatre, music and exhibitions of arts and crafts.

There's also a range of more energetic activities such as a fun run and cycling event, a kite day and Sea Week — celebrating Whangarei's intimate association with the sea.

And what better way to stage a little private celebration of that association of your own than to toast it with a glass of wine on the waterfront?

Fieldays: Mystery Creek, Hamilton, June

Fieldays? Nah, that's for tractor fiends and people wearing Drizabones and Red Bands who have a professional interest in animal breeding. It's for hayseeds and cockies, isn't it? Well, it may have started out as a trade show for the agricultural industry, but it has somewhat widened its appeal since then. And while it's still an agri-business show at heart — it's the largest fieldday in the southern hemisphere — there's plenty amongst the 1000 displays to interest the most committed city slicker. Over 115,000 visitors pass through its gates every year, and they all have, well, a field day.

The full, bewildering array of equipment and technology at the modern farmer's disposal is on display here — the state of the agriculturalist's art. So, too, are the animals on which it all depends, all up for trophies and ribbons in the stock shows. There are rides for children and entertainment for all ages, and an increasingly popular drawcard is the exhibition of inventions and innovations. New Zealand has always been an agricultural nation. The Fieldays is the single best way to stay in touch with our rural heritage.

Mission Concert: Napier, January

The Mission Estate vineyard used to supply wine exclusively to the Catholic mission and seminary at Greenmeadows, just outside of Hastings. These days, though, through an act of singularly Christian charity, they sell their excellent products to the public too, and lunch at the winery's restaurant is a Hawke's Bay highlight.

And now the vineyard is also used as the venue for an annual concert series. Blessed with a natural, grassy amphitheatre, the Mission Estate has hosted acts of an impressive calibre. Dame Kiri Te Kanawa took the main stage for the inaugural concert in 1993, and since then Dionne Warwick, Ray Charles, Kenny Rogers, Shirley Bassey, Julio Iglesias, The Beach Boys, the Doobie Brothers, The Hollies and Lulu, Engelbert Humperdinck, Sir Cliff Richard, John Farnham, The B-52s, and Rod Stewart have performed to ecstatic crowds.

It hardly seems to matter who's playing — being there is just about enough.

New Zealand International Sevens: Wellington, February

You know it's Sevens weekend in Wellington when you see Wonder Woman, six popes, Queen Elizabeth II, a wookie and a mob of burly, bearded schoolgirls wandering along Lambton Quay without attracting so much as a second glance from suited civil servants. This eclectic collective will be heading to or from the Cake Tin, otherwise known as Westpac Trust Stadium, for the International Rugby Sevens.

It's extraordinary how wholeheartedly the populace of the capital have taken the Sevens to heart. A kind of mass hysteria sets in. Everyone dresses up, and for two whole days and nights, they go mad. You can't beat 35,000 colourfully-attired lunatics, so you may as well join them. Join them spotting Colonel Sanders, as he appears among the crowd. Sing along with the Freddy Mercury lookalike. Surrender to your destiny as but a molecule in a Mexican Wave. Madly cheer the Kenyan post-match dance. And somewhere along the line, watch the sublime skills of the athletes from 16 countries playing the fast, furious cousin of rugby union that is Sevens.

Opotiki Coast Silent Movie Festival: Opotiki, September

The twenties was the heyday of the silver screen. Moving picture technology may have been in its infancy — films were invariably black and white and completely silent — but it was all new and miraculous for people at the time.

Indeed, silent movies are just as much a novelty for modern

101 MUST-DO'S FOR KIWIS

audiences, and you can experience some of the magic for yourself every year at Opotoki's De Luxe Theatre.

People dress up for the occasion — suits, pencil moustaches and hats are de rigeur for men; bonnets, false eyelashes, furs and pearls for the women. Before the curtain rises, everyone stands to sing *God Save the King*.

Then raise the curtains, cut the lights, roll the projector — it's the main feature, a period movie, expertly accompanied by one of the few silent-movie pianists in the world. It's not to be missed. After all, silence is golden.

Toast Martinborough: Martinborough, November

Martinborough was pronounced dead by a national magazine in the seventies, a prime example, so they said, of the dereliction of rural New Zealand.

But then wine came to the rescue! The gravelly, limey soils of the Wairarapa's ancient flood plain proved conducive to grape growing, and 30 years later Martinborough plays host to the country's largest celebration of la dolce vita.

Every November Wellington empties, Martinborough fills, and the wine and food flow. Most of the area's cellar doors are within an easy walk of one another, turning the event into a great, sprawling street party. It's a lovely day out, the edges of reality softened by the billowy, cushioning effect of superb Martinborough Riesling, Chardonnay and Pinot Noir accompanying the gourmet food. It's hardly surprising that tickets sell out within hours of going on sale. Get in quick, so you too can take it easy.

V8 Supercars: Pukekohe, April

There's only one place in the world outside Australia where the thrashing of big Aussie grunters — otherwise known as the V8 Supercars, based on the Ford and Holden production saloons

popular on both sides of the Tasman — can be seen around a racetrack, and that's New Zealand. Pukekohe, to be precise, although the race will be shifting to the Hamilton circuit in 2008.

One of the sport's greats is our very own Greg Murphy who races for the Holden Racing Team. So there's local interest to add an edge to what is, in any event, a spectacular day out. The noise of 20 or 30 V8s with the hammer down has to be heard — or rather felt in the pit of your stomach — to be believed, and the fast Pukekohe track, with its tight bends and stingy passing lanes, sees men and machines pushed to the limits (and on the odd fender-bending occasion, beyond them). It's high octane excitement, and global warming be damned.

Whitianga Scallop Festival: Whitianga, August

Anyone who has a taste for fresh scallops does it pretty hard when the fishery is closed. By August, however, it's open season on the critters, and probably the surest way to get hold of your quota — short of strapping on an aqualung and helping yourself — is to head to Whitianga in the Coromandel for the annual Scallop Festival.

With up to 60,000 scallops going down at this event each year, you'd think there's plenty to go round. But tickets to the festival are among the scarcest fishery resources there are: you have to get in quick. If you're among the fortunate few thousand, you'll get to sample the fruits of culinary genius as applied to scallops — macadamia-crumbed scallops, scallop sausages, scallop sushi, scallop and Chardonnay shots, scallops flambéed in Midori — to name but a few.

You'll get to watch a local shucking team in action, scallop cook-offs, celebrity chef cooking demonstrations, and there's live music to keep things kicking. It's a mouth-watering prospect.

World of Wearable Art Awards Show: Wellington, September–October

The Montana World of Wearable Art Awards show outgrew its Nelson birthplace, and shifted to Wellington in 2005. The concept, however, remains the same: to combine art and the human form, colour and movement to turn fashion into performance theatre.

The sheer imaginative virtuosity is amazing. There's never any sense that history repeats: each year's offerings are radically different from the year before, and the year before that.

Awards night is an extravagant display as the best entries — from the brash to the delicate and the rich to the strange — parade one after another in the void of the darkened stage, highlighted and complemented by the lighting and the music. It's part fashion show, comedy act, exhibition, dance and drama — unforgettable.

South Island

Alexandra Blossom Festival: Alexandra, September

A fringe benefit of being the main stonefruit growing region of New Zealand is that come spring, the orchards surrounding Alexandra are festooned with delicate white and mauve blossom. The snowy blossom against the russet tints of the tussock and the cobalt blue of that great big Central Otago sky are heartbreakingly beautiful.

The Alexandra Blossom Festival is one of the oldest celebrations in New Zealand: 2007 will see the 50th Grand Festival parade, culminating in the coronation of the 50th Festival Queen.

Back in 1957 when the inaugural Blossom Festival was held, it was a one-day event. Today, festivities last two whole weeks. Those crisp mornings, and blazing spring days . . . It's blooming marvellous.

Bluff Oyster and Southland Seafood Festival: Bluff, April

The re-opening of the season on the oyster fishery of Foveaux Strait is marked every year by a festival at the headquarters of the oyster fleet, Bluff. From what started out as a clutch of stalls in the community hall, the Bluff Oyster and Southland Seafood Festival has become a red letter day on the calendar for all New Zealand foodies.

Tens of thousands of world-famous Bluff oysters are on the menu. But even if oysters too closely resemble phlegm for your delicate sensibilities, there are Southland crayfish, salmon, paua, scallops, mussels and whitefish to tempt you as well, to say nothing of the fine wines and ales and a range of sideshows and other events incorporated for your entertainment and delight.

There is something for everyone even if it's just a taste of good old-fashioned southern hospitality. Bluff: where the world's your oyster and vice versa.

Burt Munro Challenge Rally: Invercargill, November

In 1967 Burt Munro fulfilled a life-long dream when he rode his eccentrically modified vintage Indian Scout to a world land-speed record on the Bonneville Salt Flats in Utah, United States of America. His record has never been broken, and his feat was commemorated by the box-office hit, *The World's Fastest Indian*. Munro's legend started out in Southland where he and his machine were a familiar sight to Southlanders, blatting up and down the hard sand of Oreti Beach. In November 2006, Oreti hosted the first of what is intended to be the annual Burt Munro Challenge. Besides beach races recreating the round-the-oil-drums course over which Burt used to hone his skills, there are street races, an endurance race, a speedway spectacular and much more. It's a fitting way to honour the spirit of an inspirational Kiwi.

Caroline Bay Carnival: Timaru, December–January

Ever since a wharf development in the nineteenth century created some kind of oceanographic anomaly, Timaru's Caroline Bay has been pushed further east by the spontaneous build-up of sand. Over the last century, the South Canterbury town has literally grown itself a recreation reserve.

These days, Caroline Bay is Timaru's most popular holiday spot, one which attracts thousands each summer. There's a lovely safe swimming beach backed by a grassy park featuring a maze, mini-golf, a children's paddling pool and a playground.

The annual carnival is held over the Christmas and New Year holiday season, with stalls and rides, and musical and theatrical performances in the sound shell.

Festival of Colour: Wanaka, April

One of the best things about the coming of winter in Wanaka — besides the prospect of fresh powder on Treble Cone and Cardrona of course — is the blaze of colour that the poplars, oaks and willows become in autumn. To mark the kaleidoscopic display laid on by nature, the town's Festival of Colour stages a cultural extravaganza of theatre performances, dance, film, music and cuisine, along with a line up of international writers, artists, film makers and photographers.

The festival encourages interaction and there is a strong emphasis on participation in the art forms on display. Where better to unleash your creative juices?

Festival of Flowers and Romance: Christchurch, February

In February, the blooms of the Garden City are cut for display in Christchurch's Festival of Flowers and Romance.

Besides the deployment of ikebana on a municipal scale, the festival calendar features events ranging from a wearable flower parade and photographic exhibitions to the annual debate on the nature of love. Romance is most definitely in the air — along with a lot of pollen.

Le Race: Christchurch–Akaroa, March

It says something about human nature that, blessed with some of the most congenial terrain there is for cycling, the citizens of nice, flat Christchurch should devise something so infernal as Le Race.

The French name alludes not only to the destination — our own antipodean slice of La Belle France, Akaroa — but also to its resemblance to the gut-busting mountain stage of the Tour de France.

There's some spectacular scenery to admire en route — across the Canterbury Plains and Banks Peninsula. To admire that is, if you're capable of appreciating it through the visual impairment of sweat and oxygen deprivation. The course incorporates several estimable hills, including the 571-metre Duvauchelle Peak, before dropping into Akaroa and the finish line. Saddle up and sacré bleu!

Molesworth Muster: Molesworth–Hanmer Springs, November

The rough, 80-kilometre road from Molesworth Station in inland Marlborough through to Hanmer Springs used to be used once a year to drive the station's cattle to the market. The road still closes in the winter.

These days, its busiest time of the year by far comes when the Molesworth Muster is on. Mountain bikers descend on the area en masse to ride the route. It's a tough ride, but the drama of the Kaikoura Ranges with their snow caps, their scree slopes, framing the wide, grassy river valleys, is there to soothe the soul, if not the saddle-soreness.

Nelson Jazz Festival: Nelson, January

The only thing sultrier than a Nelson summer afternoon is the combination of a jazz combo, some good food, some fine wine — and a Nelson summer afternoon.

You can have it all during the annual Nelson Jazz Festival, staged at some pretty special locations throughout the region every January. Such is the reputation of the event that it attracts international as well as local jazz men (and women). It's hot. It's cool. It's warmly recommended.

New Zealand Cup and Show Week: Christchurch, November

Whether you're a high-rolling punter with an eye for quality horseflesh, or whether the horses you follow tend to follow other horses, you'll have a ball at one of the highlights of the New Zealand racing calendar. Two major races are held during Cup Week in Christchurch, the New Zealand Cup itself and the Christchurch Casino Trotting Cup. The stakes are high, and the excitement in the grandstand is palpable.

As is customary at such events, dressing up is obligatory, and the fashion stakes are as keenly contested as anything out there on the turf. Various competitions and parades bring out the best in hats, heels and frocks.

Cup Week coincides with the Royal New Zealand Show, the biggest and best showcase of the agricultural bounty the mainland has to offer.

Otago Festival of the Arts: Dunedin, October

One of New Zealand's newest festivals of the arts is destined to become one of the best, as befits a city that celebrates 'the divine Robbie', the Hibernian Bard, Robbie Burns.

Established in 2000, the biennial Otago Festival of the Arts runs over ten days and includes upward of 40 events, featuring international, national and local practitioners of the visual, dramatic and literary kind. Och aye the noo. It's great.

Queenstown Winter Festival: Queenstown, June–July

Every year, just prior to the July school holidays and as if to get everyone in the mood for them, Queenstown holds its annual Winter Festival, beginning with a spectacular fireworks display, splashed against the Remarkables and reflected in the waters of Lake Wakatipu.

As if the town doesn't have enough going for it, the festival has become a supremely popular event with locals and tourists alike. The events emphasise fun and participation. Perhaps the Speight's Dog Derby, where dog-owners and their dogs flounder in the snow in Queenstown's winter garden, Coronet Peak, is the best of them. Perhaps that honour belongs to the Business Leaders' Drag Race. Each of the 10,000 people who rug up and watch every year will have their own opinion.

Speight's Coast to Coast: Kumara Beach–Christchurch, February

It's one of the world's great multi-sport events, but most of its competitors won't see it that way while they're en route from Kumara on the West Coast to Sumner Beach way over on the east. It's 140 gut-busting, ankle-turning kilometres from start to finish. It's run (and cycled, and kayaked) by thousands every year, both serious competitors from these shores and overseas, and by ordinary Kiwis up for the challenge. You can compete as an individual or as a member of a team: it's a supreme accomplishment, either way.

The Speight's Coast to Coast will celebrate its twenty-fifth anniversary in 2007. It's high time you joined in, I'd say.

Waipara Wine and Food Celebration: Waipara, March

A low range of hills seaward of the Waipara Valley creates a kind of microclimate there — it's consistently a couple of degrees warmer than the wine-growing areas further south. The valley itself features deep, limestone gravels in its soil structure. Yet people still thought the group of Christchurch professionals — doctors and dentists — who first planted grapes in Waipara were mad.

Well, those pioneers were right and the knockers were wrong. Waipara pinot noir is gaining a reputation as illustrious as that from Wairarapa and Central Otago.

Just how wrong the gainsayers were you can decide for yourself at the Waipara Wine and Food Celebration, where the best of the bounty of the valley and the wider Canterbury region are on display.

Wildfoods Festival: Hokitika, March

In case you have any doubts about how wild the West Coast is, there's always the menu of the Hokitika Wild Foods Festival to convince you. There was a time when a whitebait fritter or possum stew was pretty daring. Now it's anyone for fish eyes or deep-fried cicada? How about a little something done with juicy earthworms? Or deer tongue, with pistachio ice-cream to follow?

To take your mind off what's going in your gob, there's roving entertainment — live bands, solo artists, mime artists, comedy acts and stilt walkers. And Hokitika is the home of one of the world's finest beers, Monteiths Original Ale — guaranteed to wash the aftertaste of weasel burgers out of your mouth.

They're a colourful bunch down the coast. Perhaps it's true as they say, you are what you eat . . .

World Buskers Festival: Christchurch, January

Christchurch has created something pretty special in its central arts precinct, which embraces the city's museum, art gallery and markets and a number of heritage buildings. It provides a venue for the dozens of weird and wacky international and local street acts who descend upon it for the annual World Buskers Festival.

It's a decidedly user-friendly arts festival from a spectator's point of view, as there's no need to plan ahead or queue for hours to purchase tickets. The events are around every street corner, free to all.

Spontaneous fringe-style theatre breaks out without warning. The most organised thing on offer is the newly introduced 'Peep Show' — a one-of-a-kind, synchronised four-screen projection show where audiences can enter an Alice in Wonderland enclosure to see a choreographed, audio-visual display of previous festival highlights.

Don't forget to take a pocketful of change.

National

All Black Tests

By September 2007, it will have been twenty years, and that's about long enough. It's high time the William Webb Ellis Trophy came home.

It's going to be a big year for the All Blacks, as they build up to their triumphal march through the sixth World Cup in France in September and October. First, they take on France and Canada in the home series in June. Then they're playing the old foes — Australia and South Africa — in the Tri-Nations tournament in June and July.

It hardly matters where you see an All Blacks test. Just as Kiwi supporters abroad turn whichever foreign stadium they play into a little slice of New Zealand, at home we put aside parochial considerations and throw our weight in behind the Men in Black wherever we are. Whether the ABs are playing Eden Park, Waikato Stadium, the Cake Tin, Jade Stadium or the House of Pain, every one of the boys is a hometown hero.

It's one of the most intense sporting experiences anywhere, and it's coming to a stadium near you.

Black Caps International Cricket

The sun, the immaculately mown grass, the sound of willow on leather, the burble of the commentary and the polite applause — that's only in the backyards of New Zealand homes up and down the country. Those backyards empty out when there's a big game in town.

Cricket suits our lazy summers, and there's no better day out than on the terraces on the pivotal day of a Test Match that has turned out to be a scorcher.

Whether it's the ebb and flow of fortune in a five-day test, the gladiatorial duel between bat and ball before a packed stadium at a one day international, or the wham-bam form of the modern game, Twenty-Twenty, cricket is a quintessential Kiwi summer pastime.

Take a chillybin, a hat, the sunblock and an appetite for entertainment.

North Island

REGION: Northland
DURATION: 3 days
Day 1: Hundertwasser Toilets
Day 2: Hokianga and Waipoua Forest
Day 3: Bay of Islands and Waitangi Treaty Grounds

REGION: Northland
DURATION: 5 days
Day 1: Hundertwasser Toilets
Day 2: Hokianga, Waipoua Forest and Ahipara and Shipwreck Bay
Day 3: Cape Reinga
Day 4: Bay of Islands, Waitangi Treaty Grounds
Day 5: Tutukaka/The Poor Knights Islands
(Endless Summer Festival)

REGION: Auckland
DURATION: 2 days
Day 1: Visit some of the Gulf Islands
Day 2: Kelly Tarlton's and Auckland Museum plus a volcano visit (any one of 48!)

REGION: Auckland
DURATION: 5 days
Day 1: West coast: Waitakere and west coast beaches
Day 2: City sites: Sky Tower/Skyjump, Mount Eden and Auckland Zoo
Day 3: Day trip to Tiritiri Matangi

Day 4: Devonport and North Head (shopping and exploring) plus a trip to Waiheke or Rangitoto Islands
(Ellerslie Flower Show, Big Day Out, Anniversary Day Regatta, Christmas in the Park)

REGION: Waikato/Waitomo
DURATION: 2 days
Day 1: Visit to Raglan; surf city
Day 2: Underground adventure at Waitomo Caves
(Fieldays)

REGION: Franklin/Coromandel
DURATION: 5 days
Day 1: Port Waikato; sand, surf and sunsets
Day 2: Pinnacles and Kaueranga Valley; on to Coromandel Township
Day 3: New Chums Beach
Day 4: Hot Water Beach
Day 5: Karangahake Gorge
(Beach Hop, Scallop Festival)

REGION: Bay of Plenty
DURATION: 2 days
Day 1: Mount Maunganui
Day 2: White Island

REGION: Bay of Plenty/Rotorua
DURATION: 5 days
Day 1: Mount Maunganui
Day 2: White Island
Day 3: Rafting and luge
Day 4: Whakarewarewa and Te Puia (Whakarewarewa Thermal Valley)
Day 5: Mount Tarawera

REGION: Rotorua
DURATION: 2 days
Day 1: Rotorua geothermal; Hells Gate and Kaituna rafting
Day 2: Waimangu and Wai-o-tapu and Luge/Skyrides/swing

REGION: Rotorua/Taupo
DURATION: 5 days
Day 1: Rotorua geothermal; Hells Gate and Kaituna Rafting
Day 2: Luge/Skyrides/swing and Whakarewarewa
Day 3: Mount Tarawera
Day 4: Waimangu and Wai-o-tapu
Day 5: Taupo water attraction; Huka Falls/Huka Jet

REGION: Taupo/Ruapehu
DURATION: 4 days
Day 1: Orakei Korako and Huka Falls
Day 2: Taupo water attractions; Trout fishing Lake Taupo and/or Tongaririo River/rafting
Day 3: Tongariro Crossing trek
Day 4: Day skiing at Whakapapa (winter only)

REGION: Ruapehu
DURATION: 3 days
Day 1: Treks Tongariro National Park; Ruapehu, Ngauruhoe and Tongariro
Day 2: Whanganui National Park
Day 3: The Forgotten World Highway

101 MUST-DO'S FOR KIWIS

REGION: Eastland
DURATION: 5 days
Day 1: SH35 from Opotiki to Gisborne
Day 2: SH35 from Opotiki to Gisborne
Day 3: Wainui Beach and Rere Rock Slide
Day 4: Lake Waikaremoana
Day 5: Lake Waikaremoana
(Opotiki Coast Silent Movie Festival)

REGION: Hawkes Bay/Eastland
DURATION: 3 days
Day 1: Cape Kidnappers for golfing and visiting gannets
Day 2: In and around Hawke's Bay wineries including Te Mata Peak
Day 3: In and around Hawke's Bay wineries including Te Mata Peak
Day 4: Lake Waikaremoana
(Art Deco Weekend, Mission Estate Concert)

REGION: Taranaki
DURATION: 2 days
Day 1: Coast walkway and then surf
Day 2: Wilderness mountain walk or four-wheel-drive trip; Mount Taranaki

REGION: Taranaki
DURATION: 4 days
Day 1: Relax amongst the gardens of the Paradise Garden Tour
Day 2: Leisurely cycle along the oceanside — coastal walkway
Day 3: Play a game of golf and visit an artisan or gallery
Day 4: Trek on Mt Taranaki

REGION: Wanganui/Manawatu/Kapiti
DURATION: 3 days
Day 1: Visit the Whanganui National Park and the Bridge to Nowhere
Day 2: Travel to Palmerston North; Rugby Museum
Day 3: Continue road journey down the coast for trip to nature sanctuary; Kapiti Island

REGION: Wairarapa
DURATION: 2 days
Day 1: Arrange a bach and stay on the beach at Castlepoint
Day 2: Explore Cape Palliser including the historic lighthouse or try fishing at Ngawi
Day 3: Watch the sun rise (or set) at Aotearoa Stonehenge
(Toast Martinborough)

REGION: Kapiti/Wellington
DURATION: 5 days
Day 1: A trip to nature sanctuary; Kapiti Island
Day 2: Take in a debate at Parliament and tour the buildings
Day 3: Walk around the Wellington waterfront taking in the Writers' Walk and indulging in a cappuccino along the way
Day 4: Spend a day exploring our history at Te Papa
Day 5: Cruise to the Marlborough Sounds on the Interislander

REGION: Wellington
DURATION: 2 days
Day 1: Te Papa
Day 2: Parliament Buildings
(World of Wearable Art , International Sevens)

Throw in an All Black test match in Auckland or Wellington in any one of these itineraries.

South Island

REGION: **Nelson**
DURATION: 2 days
Day 1: Mountain biking Takaka Hill and Takaka township, including Port Hill
Day 2: Visit the organic farmers' market followed by spa treatment or alternative treatment session such as aromatherapy, reflexology and yoga

REGION: **Nelson**
DURATION: 5 days
Day 1–2: Trek the 51 kilometre Coastal Track at Abel Tasman National Park; visit Kaiteriteri Beach
Day 3: Take a tour on the longest natural sandbar in the world, Farewell Spit
Day 4: Afternoon mountain bike demon trip up Takaka Hill. Soak up the atmosphere of Nelson and have fish n chips on the beach at sunset
Day 5: Take in the farmers' market followed by spa treatment or alternative treatment session
(Nelson Jazz Festival)

REGION: **Marlborough**
DURATION: 3 days
Day 1–2: Marlborough Sounds: visit Havelock and Picton: fishing, diving, sailing and kayaking, hiking or

taking an eco-tour, where you can get up close to endangered wildlife
Day 3: Tour of Marlborough's vineyards

REGION: **Marlborough**
DURATION: 3–4 days
Day 1–3/4: Walk theQueen Charlotte Track

REGION: **West Coast**
DURATION: 5 days
Day 1: Travel the length and 'breadth' of the West Coast and visit Buller Gorge
Day 2: The Punakaiki 'pancake rocks' and Paparoa National Park
Day 3: Fox and Franz Josef Glaciers and Lake Matheson
Day 4: Take the road to Jackson Bay — before completing the Haast Pass
Day 5: Visit the Blue Pools of the Haast Pass
(Coast to Coast starting at Kumara Beach, Wild Foods Festival)

REGION: **West Coast**
DURATION: 2 days
Day 1: Punakaiki
Day 2: Fox and Franz Josef Glaciers and Lake Matheson

REGION: Alpine Pacific
DURATION: 2 days
Day 1: Go hard out on the mountain trails and wilderness spots around Hanmer Springs

and/or walk up Conical Hill (winter only skiing)
Day 2: Indulge in the hot pools of Hanmer Springs; include a massage
(Waipara Wine and Food Festival and Molesworth Muster)

REGION: **Hanmer Springs/ Kaikoura/Christchurch**
DURATION: 5 days
Day 1: Go hard on the mountain trails and wilderness spots around Hanmer and/or walk up Conical Hill (winter only skiing)
Day 2: Indulge in the hot pools of Hanmer Springs and include a massage
Day 3: Kaikoura for whale watching, dolphin swimming, marine exploration
Day 4: Travel to Christchurch; cycle or punt inner city
Day 5: Early morning balloon ride

REGION: **Christchurch**
DURATION: 3 days
Day 1: Day trip across the Banks Peninsula to Akaroa
Day 2: Amble around Christchurch city; cycle, punt, gardens visit
Day 3: Day trip on TranzAlpine (either return or link to end up in Greymouth)

REGION: **Christchurch**
DURATION: 5 days
Day 1–2: Banks Peninsula

Walkway
Day 3: Amble around Christchurch city; cycle, punt, gardens visit
Day 4: Early morning ballooning over the plains
Day 5: Day trip to Kaikoura

REGION: Christchurch/ Mackenzie Country/Waitaki
DURATION: 5 days
Day 1: Amble around Christchurch city; cycle, punt, gardens visit
Day 2: Drive to Tekapo; Church of the Good Shepherd and Observatory
Day 3: Continue to Mount Cook (overnight), trekking, 4WD, Tasman Glacier
Day 4: Mount Cook
Day 5: Drive beyond to Omarama and Kurow area to get to Oamaru and Moeraki Boulders
(NZ Cup and Show Week, Festival of Flowers, Le Race, World Buskers)

REGION: Dunedin
DURATION: 3 days
Day 1: City; architecture and visit around university haunts
Day 2: Otago Peninsula; Larnach Castle and albatrosses
Day 3: Day trip to Oamaru for Moeraki Boulders

REGION: Dunedin/Central Otago
DURATION: 6 days
Day 1: City; architecture and visit university haunts
Day 2: Otago Peninsula; Larnach Castle and albatrosses

Day 3–6: Taieri Gorge train to Middlemarch and connect with rail-trail-bike ride through the Maniototo to Clyde
(Otago Festival of Colour)

REGION: Queenstown
DURATION: 5 days
Day 1: Day trip from Queenstown to Maniototo for curling (Naseby)
Day 2: Relax in Queenstown; golf and *TSS Earnslaw*
Day 3: Morning exploring Arrowtown; afternoon (from 4pm) night skiing at Coronet Peak (winter only)
Day 4: Full day excursion to Glenorchy for Dart River Safaris
Day 5: Action and Adventure day

REGION: Queenstown
DURATION: 3 days
Day 1: Action and Adventure day
Day 2: Action and Adventure day
Day 3: Relax in Queenstown; golf and TSS *Earnslaw*
(Winter Festival, Alexandra Blossom Festival)

REGION: Wanaka
DURATION: 4 days
Day 1: Cross-country skiing
Day 2: Walking Lake Wanaka area including outlet track and Albert Town; stop in at Rippon for some winetasting
Day 3: Relax in Wanaka including Puzzling World
Day 4: Day trip to Haast Pass to discover hidden secrets

REGION: Wanaka/West Coast
DURATION: 3 days
Day 1: Walking Lake Wanaka area including outlet track and Albert Town; stop in at Rippon for some wine tasting
Day 2: Relax in Wanaka and include a visit to Puzzling World
Day 3: Day trip to Haast Pass to discover hidden secrets then on to West Coast
(Otago Festival of Colour)

REGION: Fiordland
DURATION: 5 days
Day 1–5: Enjoy treks in the Fiordland National Park: Milford, Kepler or Routeburn tracks
Last day: Overnight at Doubtful Sound

REGION: Fiordland
DURATION: 4 days
Day 1–3: Hollyford track
Day 4: Day trip into Milford Sound/Milford Cruise

REGION: Southland
DURATION: 3 days
Day 1–3: From Invercargill excursion north on the Southern Scenic Route to Dunedin
(Burt Munro Challenge Rally, Bluff Oyster and Southland Seafood Festival)

REGION: Southland
DURATION: 4 days
Day 1–3: Stewart Island
Day 4: Ulva Island

101 MUST-DO'S FOR KIWIS

North Island

Travelling Times and Distances

To find the distance and time needed to travel between, for example, Thames and Hicks Bay, put one finger on the name Thames and the other on the name Hicks Bay. Move sideways along the chart from Thames and upwards from Hicks Bay. Where they meet you'll see the distance between them is 414km and the travelling time is 7 hours 50 minutes. This time is for a driver travelling at 80-100 km/h on open stretches, with a small allowance for traffic delays, petrol stops and refreshments.

Times courtesy of the Ministry of Transport.

Each cell shows travelling time (hrs:mins) and distance (km).

From \ To	Whakatane	Wellington	Wanganui	Waitomo	Waikaremoana	Thames	Tauranga	Taumarunui	Taupo	Rotorua	Palmerston North	Paihia	New Plymouth	Napier	Masterton	Kaitaia	Hicks Bay	Hamilton	Gisborne	Dargaville	Whakapapa Village	Cape Reinga	Auckland
Whangarei	7:45 / 464	12:05 / 823	9:50 / 622	6:00 / 365	10:40 / 555	4:40 / 279	6:10 / 370	7:35 / 451	6:55 / 443	6:25 / 400	10:30 / 702	1:15 / 71	9:10 / 522	9:25 / 586	12:10 / 811	3:00 / 155	11:55 / 668	4:45 / 291	11:10 / 664	1:05 / 58	8:25 / 510	5:15 / 271	3:00 / 165
Whakatane		7:55 / 545	5:10 / 358	4:05 / 235	5:40 / 241	3:40 / 209	1:35 / 97	4:15 / 257	2:45 / 165	1:25 / 85	6:20 / 424	9:00 / 534	7:00 / 384	5:15 / 308	8:00 / 533	10:55 / 618	4:10 / 205	3:05 / 193	3:25 / 201	7:50 / 478	4:15 / 262	13:00 / 734	4:55 / 298
Wellington			2:45 / 195	7:10 / 473	8:00 / 506	8:20 / 586	8:00 / 546	5:15 / 371	5:10 / 380	6:30 / 460	2:10 / 145	13:20 / 894	5:10 / 355	4:50 / 323	1:50 / 102	15:05 / 978	11:55 / 718	7:30 / 532	8:15 / 538	12:10 / 838	4:45 / 344	17:20 / 1094	9:15 / 658
Wanganui				5:10 / 273	7:00 / 435	6:55 / 479	6:35 / 439	3:15 / 171	3:05 / 229	4:25 / 309	1:10 / 74	12:05 / 693	2:25 / 160	3:50 / 252	2:50 / 183	13:50 / 777	10:40 / 643	6:05 / 331	7:15 / 467	10:55 / 637	2:45 / 141	16:05 / 894	8:00 / 457
Waitomo					7:00 / 322	3:05 / 182	2:30 / 151	1:55 / 102	2:35 / 163	2:45 / 166	6:20 / 341	7:15 / 436	3:30 / 173	5:05 / 306	8:00 / 450	9:00 / 520	8:15 / 449	1:15 / 74	7:30 / 445	6:05 / 380	2:45 / 159	11:15 / 636	3:10 / 200
Waikaremoana						6:55 / 320	5:45 / 242	6:30 / 303	4:35 / 186	4:15 / 156	5:50 / 361	11:55 / 626	10:00 / 482	3:10 / 183	6:30 / 416	13:40 / 710	6:35 / 342	5:55 / 264	2:55 / 162	10:45 / 570	6:05 / 283	15:55 / 826	7:50 / 390
Thames							2:05 / 116	4:40 / 268	3:10 / 206	2:40 / 164	6:45 / 465	5:55 / 350	6:15 / 339	5:40 / 349	8:25 / 574	7:40 / 434	7:50 / 414	1:50 / 108	7:05 / 410	4:45 / 294	4:40 / 303	15:55 / 550	1:50 / 114
Tauranga								4:05 / 235	2:25 / 156	1:30 / 86	6:00 / 415	7:25 / 441	5:40 / 308	4:55 / 299	7:40 / 524	9:10 / 525	5:45 / 302	1:55 / 106	5:00 / 298	6:15 / 385	3:45 / 236	11:25 / 641	3:20 / 205
Taumarunui									1:55 / 117	2:50 / 172	4:25 / 239	8:50 / 522	3:30 / 183	4:25 / 260	6:05 / 348	10:35 / 606	8:50 / 487	2:50 / 160	7:20 / 449	7:40 / 466	0:50 / 59	12:50 / 722	4:45 / 286
Taupo										1:20 / 80	3:35 / 259	8:10 / 514	5:25 / 296	2:30 / 143	5:15 / 368	9:55 / 598	6:55 / 370	2:10 / 152	5:25 / 332	7:00 / 458	1:30 / 97	12:10 / 714	4:05 / 278
Rotorua											4:55 / 339	7:40 / 470	5:35 / 299	3:50 / 223	6:35 / 448	9:25 / 554	5:35 / 290	1:40 / 108	4:50 / 286	6:30 / 414	2:50 / 177	11:40 / 670	3:35 / 234
Palmerston North												11:45 / 773	3:35 / 234	2:40 / 178	1:40 / 109	13:30 / 857	9:45 / 573	5:45 / 411	6:05 / 393	10:35 / 717	3:10 / 223	15:45 / 973	7:40 / 537
Paihia													10:25 / 593	10:40 / 657	13:25 / 882	2:15 / 107	13:10 / 739	6:00 / 362	12:25 / 735	2:20 / 129	9:40 / 581	4:30 / 223	4:05 / 236
New Plymouth														6:15 / 412	5:15 / 343	12:10 / 677	11:10 / 589	4:25 / 231	10:25 / 585	9:15 / 537	4:20 / 242	14:25 / 797	6:20 / 357
Napier															3:20 / 233	12:25 / 744	7:05 / 395	4:40 / 295	3:25 / 215	9:30 / 601	4:00 / 240	14:40 / 857	6:35 / 421
Masterton																15:10 / 966	10:25 / 628	7:25 / 520	6:45 / 448	12:15 / 826	4:50 / 332	17:25 / 1082	9:20 / 646
Kaitaia																	14:55 / 823	7:45 / 446	14:10 / 819	3:10 / 169	11:25 / 665	2:15 / 116	5:50 / 320
Hicks Bay																		7:15 / 398	3:40 / 180	12:00 / 683	8:25 / 467	17:10 / 939	9:05 / 503
Hamilton																			6:30 / 394	4:50 / 306	3:40 / 219	10:00 / 562	1:55 / 126
Gisborne																				11:15 / 684	6:55 / 429	16:25 / 935	8:20 / 499
Dargaville																					8:30 / 525	5:25 / 285	2:55 / 180
Whakapapa Village																						13:40 / 780	5:35 / 345
Cape Reinga																							8:05 / 436

South Island

Travelling Times and Distances

To find the distance and time needed to travel between, for example, Haast and Timaru, put one finger on the name Haast and the other on the name Timaru. Move down the chart from Haast and across from Timaru. Where they meet you'll see the distance between them is 418km and the travelling time is 8 hours 10 minutes. This time is for a driver travelling at 80-100 km/h on open stretches, with a small allowance for traffic delays, petrol stops and refreshments.

Times courtesy of the Ministry of Transport.

Each cell shows travelling time (hours:minutes) over the distance in kilometres.

To \ From	Alexandra	Blenheim	Christchurch	Collingwood	Cromwell	Dunedin	Franz Josef	Geraldine	Gore	Greymouth	Haast	Invercargill	Kaikoura	Milford Sound	Aoraki/Mount Cook	Murchison	Nelson	Oamaru	Picton	Queenstown	Te Anau	Tekapo	Timaru	Twizel	Wanaka
Blenheim	11:10 / 786																								
Christchurch	6:40 / 455	4:35 / 308																							
Collingwood	16:45 / 964	4:10 / 251	7:50 / 509																						
Cromwell	0:35 / 31	10:55 / 733	6:20 / 410	16:05 / 939																					
Dunedin	3:00 / 190	9:35 / 670	5:00 / 362	12:50 / 871	3:35 / 221																				
Franz Josef	7:45 / 373	8:15 / 486	6:25 / 395	9:20 / 582	6:45 / 342	12:10 / 563																			
Geraldine	5:15 / 315	6:25 / 446	1:50 / 138	9:40 / 697	4:30 / 273	3:25 / 232	7:45 / 481																		
Gore	2:00 / 136	11:50 / 821	7:15 / 513	15:05 / 1022	2:35 / 167	2:15 / 151	7:05 / 509	5:40 / 387																	
Greymouth	9:50 / 661	5:05 / 324	4:10 / 258	6:10 / 384	9:55 / 526	8:10 / 551	3:10 / 177	5:15 / 329	10:25 / 704																
Haast	5:10 / 231	10:45 / 634	8:55 / 535	11:55 / 720	4:15 / 200	9:35 / 421	2:20 / 148	8:10 / 431	6:45 / 367	5:40 / 317															
Invercargill	2:55 / 202	12:45 / 887	8:10 / 579	16:00 / 1088	3:30 / 233	3:10 / 217	10:45 / 575	6:35 / 449	0:55 / 66	11:20 / 769	8:10 / 433														
Kaikoura	9:20 / 657	1:50 / 129	2:50 / 183	6:00 / 380	9:10 / 607	7:50 / 545	8:55 / 550	4:40 / 321	9:05 / 696	7:00 / 338	11:25 / 710	11:00 / 762													
Milford Sound	6:20 / 370	15:15 / 1081	11:35 / 773	21:55 / 1232	6:00 / 336	6:35 / 411	12:40 / 678	9:45 / 635	4:20 / 260	16:00 / 860	10:15 / 539	4:45 / 278	16:15 / 956												
Aoraki/Mount Cook	3:30 / 242	9:30 / 639	4:55 / 331	12:45 / 840	3:55 / 201	4:35 / 331	9:00 / 498	2:55 / 187	5:30 / 378	8:55 / 510	6:25 / 356	7:50 / 444	7:45 / 514	8:55 / 550											
Murchison	13:30 / 734	2:30 / 153	4:15 / 292	3:35 / 219	12:35 / 693	9:15 / 654	5:45 / 340	6:10 / 430	11:30 / 842	2:35 / 167	8:20 / 503	12:25 / 871	5:10 / 299	16:35 / 1029	9:00 / 623										
Nelson	12:55 / 865	1:45 / 116	6:15 / 424	1:45 / 135	12:35 / 786	11:05 / 469	7:45 / 562	8:05 / —	13:30 / 937	4:35 / 290	10:15 / —	14:15 / 1003	3:35 / 245	18:35 / 1146	10:30 / 755	2:00 / 129									
Oamaru	3:20 / 223	7:55 / 555	3:20 / 247	11:20 / 756	3:30 / 228	1:40 / 115	9:25 / 506	1:45 / 123	3:55 / 266	7:30 / 443	7:00 / 376	4:50 / 332	6:10 / 430	8:15 / 526	3:55 / 216	7:35 / 539	9:35 / 671								
Picton	11:40 / 791	0:25 / 28	5:00 / 336	4:20 / 245	11:20 / 761	10:00 / 698	8:40 / 531	6:55 / 474	12:15 / 849	5:30 / 352	11:10 / 671	13:10 / 915	2:15 / 157	18:25 / 1108	9:45 / 687	2:55 / 191	2:10 / 110	8:20 / 583							
Queenstown	1:30 / 93	11:50 / 794	7:15 / 486	17:05 / 961	0:55 / 62	4:25 / 283	7:45 / 404	6:10 / 346	2:35 / 169	10:55 / 583	5:10 / 262	3:00 / 187	11:10 / 669	5:05 / 291	3:50 / 263	11:30 / 775	13:30 / 910	4:50 / 319	13:20 / 822						
Te Anau	4:00 / 249	13:50 / 960	9:15 / 652	19:50 / 1117	3:40 / 217	4:15 / 290	10:30 / 560	7:25 / 516	2:00 / 139	13:40 / 739	7:55 / 418	2:25 / 152	13:55 / 835	2:20 / 121	6:30 / 429	14:15 / 944	16:15 / 1025	5:55 / 404	16:05 / 988	2:45 / 170					
Tekapo	3:35 / 227	7:55 / 534	3:20 / 226	11:10 / 785	3:00 / 196	4:30 / 303	9:15 / 485	1:30 / 88	5:35 / 363	6:00 / 417	6:40 / 343	6:55 / 429	6:10 / 409	9:35 / 532	1:25 / 99	7:25 / 518	9:35 / 650	2:50 / 188	8:25 / 562	5:00 / 258	6:40 / 428				
Timaru	4:40 / 307	6:45 / 471	2:10 / 163	10:00 / 672	4:25 / 268	2:50 / 199	10:45 / 493	0:35 / 35	5:05 / 350	5:20 / 352	8:10 / 418	6:00 / 416	5:00 / 346	9:25 / 610	3:10 / 203	6:25 / 455	8:25 / 587	1:10 / 84	7:10 / 499	5:35 / 335	7:05 / 489	1:40 / 104			
Twizel	2:40 / 169	8:50 / 592	4:15 / 284	12:05 / 843	2:05 / 138	3:45 / 261	7:30 / 427	2:25 / 146	4:40 / 316	6:55 / 475	5:35 / 285	6:00 / 371	7:05 / 467	8:05 / 474	0:50 / 63	8:20 / 576	10:30 / 708	2:05 / 146	9:15 / 620	3:00 / 200	5:45 / 370	0:55 / 58	2:35 / 162		
Wanaka	1:25 / 86	11:20 / 745	6:30 / 424	15:10 / 839	0:50 / 55	4:25 / 276	5:55 / 287	5:25 / 286	3:25 / 222	9:05 / 469	3:20 / 145	4:40 / 285	9:20 / 607	6:55 / 394	3:00 / 203	10:45 / 715	12:45 / 848	3:40 / 231	11:45 / 773	1:50 / 117	4:35 / 273	— / —	4:35 / 198	2:15 / 140	
Westport	11:35 / 761	4:15 / 264	5:10 / 333	5:20 / 320	11:45 / 639	10:55 / 695	4:55 / 277	7:45 / 432	12:10 / 804	1:45 / 101	7:30 / 437	13:05 / 869	5:30 / 340	16:05 / 951	10:00 / 664	1:45 / 101	3:45 / 226	8:30 / 580	4:40 / 288	12:30 / 664	14:30 / 830	14:10 / 559	8:05 / 497	9:25 / 617	10:45 / 558

Northland

Ahipara and Shipwreck Bay: surf's up **A**
Bay of Islands: where beauty knows no bounds **SS/A**
Cape Reinga: sand, surf and spirits **SS**
Hokianga: changing your clock to Hokianga Time **HT**
Hundertwasser Toilets: the loo that made headlines **HT/AC**
Tutukaka/The Poor Knights Islands: underwater utopia **HT/SS**
Waipoua Forest: kauri kings **HT/SS**
Waitangi Treaty Grounds: the story of our past, present and future **HH**

Auckland

Animal Crazy: up close and personal with marine and wildlife **F**
Auckland Gulf Islands: Waiheke, Great Barrier, Rangitoto and Tiritiri Matangi Islands **SS**
Auckland Volcanoes: you haven't seen Auckland until you've checked out its cones **SS**
Auckland War Memorial Museum: bringing memories, treasures and learning to life **AC/HT**
Auckland's West Coast: a sanctuary on the city's doorstep **SS**
Devonport and North Head: from fortification site to charming seaside village **HH**
Skyjump and Sky Tower: views from inside and outside Auckland's Sky Tower **F**

Franklin

Port Waikato: sand, surf and sunsets **HT/SS**

Waikato

Raglan: Waikato's surf 'city' **A/S**

Waitomo

Waitomo Caves: underground — soft and hard adventure **A/HT**

Coromandel

Coromandel Township: explore the unique art scene **HH/AC**
Hot Water Beach: sandy excavation on the Coromandel coast **HT/I**
Karangahake Gorge: a window into our mining past **HH**
New Chums Beach: Coromandel's shy superstar **HT**
The Pinnacles: become Lord of the Pinnacles in the Kaueranga Valley **HH/SS**

Bay of Plenty

Mount Maunganui: Mauao: the story of Mauao, his tracks and beaches **A/SS**
White Island: New Zealand's only active marine volcano **A/SS**

Rotorua

Mount Tarawera: from eruption to eco-action **HH/A/SS**
Rotorua Geothermal: heaven and hell combined **I/SS**
Rotorua Luge, Skyrides and Skyswing: what goes up, must come down **A**
Rotorua Rafting: raft the mighty Kaituna River **A**
Whakarewarewa: Keeping traditional Maori villages, arts and culture alive **AC/HH**

Taupo

Lake Taupo's Top Water Attractions: trout fishing, cascading falls and Tongariro River **A/S/SS**
Orakei Korako: Taupo's hidden treasures **A/S/SS**
Tongariro Crossing: walking the heritage line **A/HH**

Ruapehu

Ruapehu, Ngauruhoe and Tongariro: the North Island's sacred mountains **A/SS**
The Forgotten World Highway: remembering the past **HH**
Whanganui National Park: home of the Whanganui River **SS**

Eastland

Eastland: New Zealand's scenic coastal road journey **HH/CS**
Lake Waikaremoana: Te Urewera National Park: Children of the Mist **A/SS**
Rere Rock Slide: Gisborne's natural rock slide **A**
Wainui Beach: chardonnay sunrise **I/SS**

Hawke's Bay

Cape Kidnappers: gannets and golf; par excellence **S/SS**
Fine wine: fabulous food **I**
Te Mata Peak: the looming legend **SS**

Taranaki

Taranaki Gardens in paradise tour: heaven for garden lovers **SS**
Mount Taranaki: from mountain snow to surf in a day **SS/A**
New Plymouth's coastal walkway: a walk on the oceanside **SS**

Wanganui

The Bridge to Nowhere: Whanganui National Park **HT**

Manawatu

NZ Rugby Museum: a shrine to the oval ball **HH/S**

Wairarapa

Cape Palliser: nature's power **SS**
Castlepoint: old-fashioned seaside adventure **F**

A	Adventure	**F**	Family	**I**	Indulgence
AC	Art/Culture	**HH**	Heritage/History	**S**	Sport
E	Events	**HT**	Hidden Treasure	**SS**	Scenic Splendour

Stonehenge Aotearoa: marking the winter solstice down under **HT**

Kapiti
Kapiti Island: flora and fauna sanctuaries **SS/HT**

Wellington
Beehive and Parliament buildings: peeking into the corridors of power **AC/HH**
Te Papa Tongarewa: New Zealand's national museum in Wellington **AC/HH**
The Interislander experience: cruising between the islands **SS**
Wellington's Writers' Walk: wordsmiths of the capital **AC**

Nelson
Abel Tasman National Park: world-renowned kayaking and marine reserve **SS**
Farewell Spit: the south's super-size hook **F/A/SS**
Seafood City: enjoy the catch of the day **SS/I**
Spa and well-being destination: soothing massage **I**
Takaka Hill: Rameka Track: mountain mecca for mountain bike demons **S/A**

Marlborough
Marlborough Sounds: sea-lover's sanctuary **SS**
Marlborough Wine Trail: wine tasting and gourmet delights **I**
The Queen Charlotte Track: fit for a Queen **HH/SS**

West Coast
Buller Gorge: the power of water **F/SS/A**
Fox and Franz Josef Glaciers: relics of the last Ice Age **SS**
Lake Matheson: reflecting the mighty Aoraki Mount Cook **SS/HT**

Punakaiki: home of the famous Pancake Rocks **F/SS**
South Westland: a World Heritage listed location **SS**

Alpine-Pacific Triangle
Hanmer Springs: it's not just hot water you can throw yourself into **I/A**

Canterbury
Akaroa and Banks Peninsula: a hint of French charm **F/HH/SS**
Arthur's Pass National Park: the great alpine railway **F/HH/SS**
Canterbury Plains Hot Air Ballooning: float where the breeze may take you **SS/I**
Christchurch City: cycling, kayaking and punting through the Garden City **HH/SS/F/S**
Coastal Kaikoura: the ultimate marine destination **F/SS**

MacKenzie Country
Aoraki/Mount Cook: alpine majesty **A/S**
Lake Tekapo: observatory and Church of the Good Shepherd **HH/SS**

Waitaki
Moeraki Boulders: steroids, dinosaur droppings, or space craft ball bearings? **SS**

Dunedin
Dunedin City: architecture and the 'scarfie' experience **HH/AC**
Otago Peninsula: wicked wildlife and castles **HT/SS/HH**

Central Otago
Central Otago Curling: broom . . . and 'crack an egg' **HT/F/S**
Otago Rail Experience: all aboard for the Rail and Bike Trail **F/HH/SS**
Queenstown
Arrowtown: born of gold **F/SS/HH**

Glenorchy and Dart River: venture into the wilderness **SS/A**
Golf in an Alpine Amphitheatre: take your camera with your clubs **SS/S**
Queenstown Adventure: extreme pursuits in an extreme environment **A**
TSS Earnslaw: the Lady of the Lake **HH/F/SS**
Winter Mountain Fun: night skiing and riding **F/S/A**

Wanaka
Cross-Country Skiing: enjoy the tranquility on the Pisa Range **S**
Kicking the Autumn Leaves: along the banks of the Clutha headwaters **SS**
Puzzled World: world of conundrums in Lake Wanaka **F/A**
The Blue Pools of Haast Pass: discover forest secrets **HT**

Fiordland
Doubtful Sound: waking up in a fiord **HT/SS**
Fiordland National Park: Great Walks **A/SS**
Hollyford Valley: Fiordland gourmet **SS/I**
Mitre Peak and Milford Sound: magnificent Milford **SS**

Southland
Southern Scenic Route: taking in the wild wild South **SS**
Stewart Island: the great Southland escape **SS**
Ulva Island: hear the famed dawn chorus **SS/A**

Go Camping
Camping Country: every nook and cranny hides a camping spot **F**

Attend a Must-do Event **E**

A	Adventure	F	Family	I	Indulgence
AC	Art/Culture	HH	Heritage/History	S	Sport
E	Events	HT	Hidden Treasure	SS	Scenic Splendour

101 MUST-DO'S FOR KIWIS

Thanks to the following organisations who helped bring this campaign to you.

101 MUST-DO'S FOR KIWIS

Glossary

bach/crib a weekend or beach cottage
hapu sub-tribe/clan
iwi tribe
kai moana seafood
kuia old lady
mana integrity/prestige
mirimiri stroke
patupaiarehe fairy/nymph
pounamu greenstone
tangata whenua local people/native
Te Ao Maori Maori world
tipuna ancestor
waharoa gateway to pa (stockaded village)
waka canoe

101 MUST-DO'S
FOR KIWIS